Garden doctors

Gardendoctors

New Ideas for Planning and Planting

Dan Pearson and **Steve Bradley**

 B⊞XTREE

in association with

 Magazine

A CHANNEL FOUR BOOK

First published in Great Britain in 1996 by Boxtree Limited

1 2 3 4 5 6 7 8 9 10

Designed by **DW Design**
Printed and bound in the UK by Bath Press Colourbooks, Glasgow, for

Boxtree Limited
Broadwall House
21 Broadwall
London SE1 9PL

A CIP catalogue entry for this book is available from the British Library.

ISBN 0 7522 1029 7

Jacket photographs:
Front jacket (bottom three), front flap and back jacket by Andrea Jones
Front jacket (top) and back flap by Des Willie
Front jacket illustration by Nick Pearson

Garden Doctors: New Ideas for Planning and Planting accompanies the Channel Four programme 'Garden Doctors' produced by Flashback Television Limited.

Contents

Introduction

In **these days** of ever-shrinking gardens, we demand more and more from our little patch of nature. We want year-round colour, greater production of flowers and vegetables, and, perhaps most important of all, some privacy, a safe haven where we can escape and forget about all our other pressures.

As a result, the garden represents an investment, not just in terms of money but also in terms of time and effort, and, like any other investment, the reward will be greater if some research and planning is done first.

Many families look upon the garden as an extension of the house, a 'room outside', but we should never make the mistake of thinking that we can domesticate the plants we are using. If they are big in their natural habitat, then they will be big in the garden too, and if they naturally occur on acid soil, then they will not survive on chalk.

Gardens all too often develop in a piecemeal fashion. Plants are introduced at random, often by different people, and what suited a previous owner is not necessarily going to suit you. Keen gardeners will always get sidetracked by plants which catch their eye, and without a basic design this can lead to confusion. You need to consider whether you want to change all or just part of the garden, and what you will want from it.

Identifying your requirements will help you clarify your thoughts, something which is equally important whether you are planning the garden yourself or employing a professional designer. Once this has been done, you will be in a better position to assess how much work will be involved, and what, if anything, you wish to keep.

Will you need:
- room for children's play equipment?
- a fruit- or vegetable-growing area?
- a greenhouse?
- access to the washing line or dustbin?
- screening from a neighbour or busy road?
- a low-maintenance garden?
- a patio or barbecue area?

Obviously a major factor at this stage is cost. Which parts of the work can you do yourself? If the garden is large or the project is an expensive one, you might consider dividing the work into several smaller sections, carried out over a longer period of time. This is far better than choosing a plan which could be completed more quickly at a lower cost but which you are not completely happy with.

Your new design may involve some hard landscaping – a path or paved area, walls, or perhaps an ornamental brick edging to a border – and these need to be finished before you can start planting. One point which must be stressed here is that you should take great care when using hired equipment such as chainsaws or stone-cutters. Your local hire-shop will be happy to advise you on what equipment to hire and how to use it safely.

The Channel Four series 'Garden Doctors' looked at gardens ranging in location from Nottinghamshire in the north to Cornwall in the south-west. Each garden had its own characteristics and problems, but in each case the formula described above was followed. The owner(s) of the gardens assessed what they wanted from the finished design, explained their aims to the team, which included Dan Pearson (designer), Steve ('Brad') Bradley (horticultural consultant), and the production company, in order to produce a workable plan, bearing in mind the constraints of cost and the time allowed for making the programmes. Taking into account the soil type, the location and aspect of the garden and the requirements of the owners, Dan could then create a design which Brad could begin to bring to life.

The 'Garden Doctors' series aims to provide new ideas for planning and planting your garden, as well as practical guidelines on how to approach design and construction. It follows the entire process of transformation undergone by each featured garden: the initial ideas of the owners and the notes taken by Dan, a description of each garden and its particular problems (and how they were solved), the clearing and preparation of the site, the hard landscaping, and finally the soft landscaping, planting and finishing off.

This accompanying book, *Garden Doctors: New Ideas for Planning and Planting*, also follows each of the gardens through from design to completion but covers each aspect of the work in much greater detail. The chapter 'Design and Planning' covers a

basic general approach to designing, and describes how to draw up your own plan. The materials to use, and step-by-step guidelines for technique, are discussed in detail in the chapter 'Hard Landscaping'. Many of the different materials used in the gardens are discussed, together with the reason each was chosen for a specific use. Methods of construction are also covered, although not in the kind of detail found in a specialist book on the subject. For instance, it would be difficult in a book of this size to describe the various mortar mixes which could be used when laying bricks or paving, with their advantages and disadvantages. Most good DIY stores will have information on construction, should you wish to pursue it further (and see the list of further reading on page 218).

Each garden is described individually in terms of soil type, growing conditions, whether it was hot, wet, windy, stony or just in need of a complete overhaul. The plants used are listed in each case, so that if a particular garden appealed, or was relevant to your own circumstances, you can easily find out what plants were used there, with ideas for good planting combinations.

It is difficult in a half-hour programme to show the construction of a garden which has actually taken several days to complete, and things inevitably get left out. These are the areas we have tried to cover in more detail in this book – the explanations and advice which may be glossed over a little too quickly to follow in the programme, but which will make all the difference to your own creation.

Design and Planning

1

Gardens are one of the most dynamic man-made environments. Encompassing sound, light, movement, scent, colour, texture, form, architecture and the fluctuation of nature itself, they are ideal places for the meeting of different minds and creative disciplines. Whether it be a derelict piece of land with the rough forms of demolished buildings and billowing buddleja or the inner recesses of a wooded glade, inspiration can be found all around us.

Although they are controlled environments, gardens have taken their influence from the natural environment for centuries – the stylized forms found in a thousand-year-old Chinese temple garden, for example, or the wild and naturalistic plantings of today as a response to our ever-decreasing landscapes. The natural environment is one of the richest sources of design inspiration available. It provides us with the most logical and exquisite plant combinations: tall, vertical foxgloves pushing through a froth of cow parsley, or pincushions of thrift amid drifts of bronzed heather. The texture, colour and form are all there, along with a practicality which means that a plant will only grow in a position which suits it. The richness of natural vegetation can be the source of ideas for manipulated plantings in the garden, reflected in the use of longer-performing garden varieties or plants with a similar feel or requirements. Grassland communities have influenced the free-form plantings of today,

▶ *Brad and Dan monitoring progress in the Gulf-Stream garden in Cornwall.*

▼ *Garden structures should always be bold and simple to allow room for more detail in the planting.*

with drifts of one group of plants being broken and linked with swathes of another. Even motorway embankments can inspire, with movements of white ox-eye daisies in June and stiff black teasels in winter.

Nature holds no boundaries with colour. A purple knapweed may rise from yellow buttercups. Indeed it is hard to find anything which will 'clash', and lessons can be learned from looking at what combinations are growing right up to the garden gate. The natural environment also provides us with a richness of landforms and environments which strike a balance and a harmony. Taking a look around us is enough of a lead in many situations. The soft rounded forms of sand dunes with their bleached-out vegetation can inspire a planting for a dry site, and the wetlands alongside ditches and rivers a planting for a wild pond.

Geography can influence the choice of materials used in a garden. A woodland site may demand a soft approach, an open barren site a reference to the skyscapes and the horizon. Perhaps a series of verticals, inspired by the upright growth of teasels, would be appropriate here as contrast and relief.

Even in urban situations local materials may demand an attention to detail. A tall, hard wall can become a backdrop of greenery and a soft boundary. The planting for a roof garden may take the colours of the sky and the rooftops as reference.

Inspiration for creating a garden may well come from experiences or events from the past: the memory of a childhood den in a hedge can lead to the decision to design a solitary private retreat, a grandparent who grew vegetables to a modern potager. A garden can be inspired by a textile, the plants twining through each other in richly textured layers. It could be inspired by a painting or an experience abroad – a Mediterranean arbour for shade with vines and figs.

Alternative ways of looking at materials may well come up with something interesting. Woven galvanized mesh from a builder's merchant can be used as a screen, or a climbing net from an army surplus shop as support for climbers. Lateral thinking and an open mind are the keys to a freer approach in gardening. You don't have to rely simply on what is presented to you by the trade.

Your garden should be your own personal expression and whatever form it takes, from an unkempt wilderness to an exacting, precision-orientated formality, it is all about particular tastes, needs and philosophies. Beauty is very much in the eye of the beholder and function is completely owner-specific.

Designing a garden is not an exercise in *random* personal expression, however; it should also be about creating a user-friendly place to play or relax or to indulge obsessions or fantasies. A garden provides an opportunity to create your own tailor-made environment to suit the amount of time you intend to spend in it. For some it may be a place to relax and to enjoy the company of friends and family; for others it may be a reclusive and private space. A garden can be a place to unwind physically, tending plants, digging, pruning. It can also be a place which is good for the soul, a focus in a busy world and a place to indulge the senses, with cool, soft grass underfoot, the rustle of leaves or the smell of blossom.

Once you have made the decision to tackle your outside space, one of the primary tasks is to establish the focus of the garden. This will set up the parameters of whether you will need a play lawn or a patio or other divisions in your garden, which could mean it has the potential to be divided up into rooms in much the same way that a house would be. It is, after all, an extension of your living space.

A garden has to be about its owners or inhabitants and this link between the two is essential for it to really work as living space. The link may be the owners' emotional needs, which can be a romantic escape or a desire to tend and nurture, or it may be an experimental place for creative ideas which are difficult to realize in other walks of life, or both. It can be designed as a labour-saving space for the busy professional or an on-going development for the enthusiast looking to collect, expand and move on from one area of horticulture and design into the next. It does not have to be highly organized and labour-intensive. It might simply be a space to sit or a place to grow and tend.

A garden is an ever-changing and dynamic place which is never the same from one year to the next, just as seasonal fluctuations are dramatic and intense, highlighted by the ebb and flow of growth. It provides an opportunity to establish a link with the natural world. Gardens are the ideal places to indulge our own expressions, whether these are a desire to impose order or an impulse to make some contact with a freer side of ourselves.

Each situation has its own list of pros and cons. It may have wonderful views and fearsome winds, it may have a benign and gentle climate and yet be on a slope of virtually 45 degrees. The key to creating a successful garden is to seek out the potential, the essential clue which will give the garden its spirit and individuality. It may be to do with tapping into and enhancing the *genius loci*, the natural sense of place, or it may be an imposed ideal in a place which needs a direction and a sense of escapism.

As our lives become increasingly busy, the escape routes available to us are more and more important. Tapping into what makes you tick is the starting point. Gardens are highly eclectic places, rules are set up only to be broken. Breaking with convention is often the most energizing and exciting route – why have a lawn when ground-cover planting would be more exciting and labour-saving? Imagine a vertical garden clothing the wall of an inner-city building, or a garden where all the plants are edible, an eclectic mix of fruit and vegetables and flowers where leeks are ornamental and lettuces are allowed to bolt and flower among frothy asparagus. Remember that a garden can be anything you want it to be. Borders can be restructured to resemble free-form meadows of grasses, and garden perennials and the most common plants can be used innovatively to give them a new life in the gardener's eye. With a leap of courage, conventions can be left behind or incorporated in new ways so that restrictions are hurdled and one's personal vistas can be realized.

The hard structures of a garden are just as flexible and open to personal expression as the planting and the layout of the garden itself. The hard materials you need in order to put down paths can be improvised and pulled together, salvaged, and even home-made. A fence can be constructed from split stakes and a tree can become the supports for a tree house as an escape and a lookout – for children and adults alike. Local materials may be the answer to your walling problems, or re-using inherited materials and simply treating them differently to create another aesthetic – a broken slate path from an old roof or benches made from railway sleepers. Providing the design of the garden works, the aesthetics can be driven purely by one's own personal desires. Gardens can be as free and spirited or as tended and manicured as you wish them to be. Gardening can be as intense and therapeutic as the best hours spent as a child making mud pies. They are places for the mind, the body and the spirit.

The Importance of Having a Plan

Producing an overall design for your garden is important because it will give your ideas and the garden a focus. A plan can give you the chance to complete a design over several planting seasons so that your garden develops to a pattern, however long it takes to come together and without the aims and objectives getting lost along the way. Although it may at first seem a little daunting, it is worth remembering that a plan is simply an organization of space, ideas and raw materials, i.e. the structures and the plants. One of the first steps to be made before working up a plan is to brainstorm together a list of likes and dislikes. The points can be as precise or as abstract as you want. Often dislikes will spark off a series of likes and vice versa. It is a freeing up exercise which will help to establish what you really want out of the garden. Often initial gut feelings are the most pertinent and for this reason worth putting at the top of the list. As a result, you will start to piece together an idea with a flavour and function. For instance, in our shady woodland garden Meri wanted to bring the wood up closer to the house and to make the garden feel part of the land beyond her boundaries. She knew she loved white flowers and plants with a woodland feel; she wanted to stay away from strong colour. She also knew that in reality she had to cater for her family, so a lawn for play and relaxation was necessary. These were all strong clues that helped with the design process. This is the first step of the plan.

The second step is to organize these ideas and put them together in a way that makes them begin to

◀ **Dan and Louise discuss the next stage of the Cotwolds garden.**

relate to each other as a whole. Decisions should be made about how much space should be devoted to a terrace and how to get from the terrace to the lawn. Views or focal points and how they should be highlighted are important considerations at this stage. These are all basic points which a plan merely draws together. It can be a simple sketch about space to help you resolve the area in your mind or it can be a more detailed map of plantings, a useful record and a starting point to help you work up numbers and dimensions. A plan is a place to make the first mistakes and to resolve one's thoughts and preferences. A plan will bring all the elements together in a coherent form before committing them to the ground itself.

Whether you are renovating an existing garden or starting from scratch, it is worth remembering that the simplest ideas and solutions are often the most effective. A good strong bone structure where the basic hard elements are bold and well-proportioned will mean that you can lay detail over the top with the planting to soften and embroider. Sound ergonomics are another point of importance in the construction of a successful garden. Lines of desire, the logical route across a piece of land, should be established early on, both to avoid cutting across beds and to relieve excessive wear on lawns. Focal points and divisions of designated spaces should be thoroughly thought out, and areas to store tools, dustbins or compost heaps should be carefully considered. Privacy may be a prime objective, or the opening up of a view, or the inclusion of a neighbour's tree or distant greenery beyond your boundary, may be something that could increase the potential of your garden. Many of these issues can be resolved through a little thought and careful consideration.

The next stage is to look closely at the actual

garden – what features should be retained or enhanced, what elements should be altered? Sarah and Oliver wanted to create a garden with a feeling of the wild about it, using native species to blend into the countryside. A series of conversations led quickly to the theme and motivation behind the garden. The pond should be enlarged and two distinct areas put down to wildflowers.

Equipped with a basic knowledge and an initial concept, the fourth stage is to measure out the space. First measure the boundaries and plot them on a pad so that you lay down the basic perimeter of the garden. The house, which is generally the dominant feature, should also be measured. A right-angle taken from a main wall and laid along the length of the garden will provide you with a reference point from which individual trees and features can be mapped. Canopies of trees should be plotted in addition to their trunks to establish areas of light and shade, and a compass reading included to determine north and south.

Once the main dimensions have been plotted on paper, lists of initial responses should be noted. A larchlap fence might need raising with trellis, there might be a neighbouring house that needs screening or a tree-trunk which could become a focal point. A greenhouse, for instance, should be placed so that its ridge runs east/west and away from overhanging trees. Take photographs as reference. The information you have gathered can then be laid out on to grid paper to a scale appropriate to the site. The space that you are dealing with will then become clear, and the list of features that you have noted down can be introduced. It is easy to be scared of breaking into the body of a space, however, and ergonomics are of prime importance at this stage – for a garden to work it should be easy to traverse.

Paths and terraces should therefore be generous and clear. A good plan is based on logic. Be bold: divide the garden into its basic compartments starting with the elements which are of most importance to you. Mapping out a garden which feels generous in its proportions is always easier on paper without the clutter of visual interference. This is where photographs can be used as a prompt – and if you find the process of drawing difficult, lay a sheet of tracing paper over the photograph and sketch in your proposed features over the top.

There are various devices which can help to create a greater illusion of space. For instance, in Robin's garden in Balham the inherent problem was that the garden was long and narrow. We gave the illusion of greater width by placing wood in the paving which ran across the plot. If we had run the lines lengthways, the problem would only have been exacerbated. We also created one really decent space with the square, brick terrace midway along the length of the garden, so that there was at least one area which did not feel compromised by the size of the garden. Blurring the boundaries is another device worth remembering – a solid object placed at the perimeter of a garden will only highlight the garden's boundary. A soft, lacy screen of foliage that you can just see through, which filters light and the area beyond, will give an illusion that the garden goes beyond this point. In Robin's garden the bamboo served this purpose, as well as the light and airy plantings along all the boundaries.

There are endless permutations and solutions to the problems surrounding spaces but it is worth remembering that the most effective tend to be the boldest and most simple. For instance, your site may seem impossible or difficult to use, or it may be an inhospitable slope, but in Judy and Ciarán's garden in

Cornwall we used this to advantage, creating a terrace with a decking platform as a seating area to view the garden and the sea. Steps linking the road to the deck and the deck to the jungle garden below bridged the levels and provided the garden with practical access and a route which utilized the full space. The steep bank which had previously existed was both difficult to garden and hard to negotiate on foot, and although terracing the site at first seemed daunting, it was an ideal solution to make a sloping garden into a more practical space. In Wendy and Leslie's garden in Sussex there was the same problem but to a lesser degree, and there the bank was made into a sheer drop by the new terracing – a device not only to distinguish the area from the landscape beyond but also as a matter of practicality to keep out rabbits and to provide an opportunity to increase the soil depth, which was little more than a gravel bank.

In the shade garden, Meri wanted to link the garden with the wood beyond. She also wanted a terrace as a dry area outside the house. To keep it in proportion with the house, its depth had the same measurement as the face of the house up to the gutter: a general guideline which in most situations works as a device to create comfortable proportions. This terrace was based on a grid of gravel and brick, which provided an ordered contrast to the far woodland in the vicinity of the house. As with most of the schemes, we chose to retain the most ornamental and man-made structures to the immediate area around the house, so that as you moved away from the building the natural world began to dominate. Providing a link between the house and the wood with a path or a focal point such as an urn or, as in Meri's case, the tree house, gives the garden a narrative and a lead to link the areas.

A sense of mystery is one of the most delightful elements of a garden and in most situations it is advantageous to screen part of it, whether partially or completely, to give a sense of expectation and intrigue and, above all, an area of privacy. This is often a means of creating a greater illusion of space – the mind is fooled into thinking there is something beyond. In Kirsten's garden in Norwich, we built a partial screen which divided the top third of the garden off and yet allowed views through to the wild garden beyond. It was also a way of helping to separate two distinctly different areas of interest. In Andy and Louise's family garden the working potager was divided off and kept close to the house; dividing the area up gave a greater feeling of space and provided the garden with chapters of interest. The concept was also a simple solution to the problem of safety for the children – the division of space meant that they were encouraged to play further down the garden, away from the road.

There are certain functional areas which should also be given careful consideration in the early stages of planning. Compost bins, for instance, are best placed away from the house, but not so far away that they are little used. The same applies to greenhouses and sheds. Divisions and screening can be used to conceal them; or, as an alternative, a feature such as a piece of topiary or an urn placed to one side can act as a distraction. In Robin's garden, as well as positioning bamboo to give the illusion of greater space beyond, we used it to screen the dustbins and the bottom gate, and built a deck to cover a manhole cover. However, be careful you do not draw attention to the object you are trying to conceal. Telegraph poles highlighted with clematis or bright variegated ivies are a good example of what not to do.

In the case of screening undesirables it is often

*◄ (Previous spread) **When planting a garden which is heavily influenced by its environment, as with this coastal site in east Sussex, it is vital to choose plants which are adapted to the conditions.***

best to filter out the object gently with lacy planting in much the same way as you would on a boundary. Silver birch or cut-leaved elder are good examples of plants which will 'break up' an eyesore. If you plan to cover the object with climbers, use green foliage that will blend into the background rather than flowering climbers which will focus attention.

Establishing whether the garden should be high- or low-maintenance is one of the first priorities. Creating a garden which will rule you completely may not be what you are intending, so think carefully about the relationship between planted areas and areas of paving. Try to work out how many hours per week or per month you can spend on the garden. This is an essential guide in the early planning, and should determine the elements to be included in the design. It is worth remembering that a lawn will equal many hours of maintenance over a year; and the same can be said of hedges, especially fast-growing varieties such as privet and the dreaded 'Leylandii' which has the potential to soar to 100ft (30m) in thirty years and should be avoided at all costs. There are ways of cutting down on labour if you do require a lawn, such as creating a simple mowing-edge of wood or paving up to which the mower can run, thus cutting time spent trimming edges, or, as in Sarah and Oliver's case, rough-cut and meadow areas. If all you want is greenery, think about having bed space with time-saving ground cover or put the area down to gravel and interplant with informal perennials. It may ultimately be by far the best solution.

There are certain types of plants which are higher-maintenance – annuals, for instance, are particularly time-consuming if planted on their own. Containerized gardens will also take up more time with watering, and a general rule here is to use as large a container as you can afford – the greater root space and volume of soil will dry out less rapidly. Roses are well-known for their high labour requirements – it may be better to choose the less fussy shrub and species roses. The ideal low-maintenance scheme would assure that the ground is always covered with plants and/or mulch and that successive layers of interest – from trees to shrubs to perennials to ground cover – are selected for their longevity and ability to look after themselves. Choosing the right plant for the right space is half the battle.

Thorough groundwork in the early stages of garden planning will save hours if not years of wasted effort. Local research and checking up on what the neighbours have achieved and can grow is the simplest guide, and looking at the area for inspiration can often give you a lead for the layout and the design.

Before work starts it is imperative that the garden is cleared of all perennial weeds, either manually or with an application of systemic weedkiller. A clean palette will save hours of labour at a later date. Thorough soil preparation, which should include the incorporation of organic matter such as manure, leaf-mould or compost, is another essential (see the section on soil preparation in the 'Soft Landscaping' chapter). Plants will thrive on good preparation and the garden as a whole will be realized literally twice as fast as a garden where initial preparation has been less than rigorous. Careful selection of plants to be retained is another task worth considering carefully in the early stages. Although it may seem brutal, it is

often best to remove or reduce inappropriate specimens. In Judy and Ciarán's garden in Cornwall, we decided to keep but considerably reduce the rhododendron because it stabilized the bank and provided the initial backdrop. We also chose to retain a large escallonia for wind protection despite the fact that it was not ideal for the site. Everything else which was not in keeping with a subtropical theme, such as the buddleja and the deutzia, was removed. It is often better to be rigorous at the outset and replant with your own ideas rather than to compromise and have to live with that compromise for ever. An open mind, courage and initiative are the keys to a successful garden.

'Doctored' Gardens

2

One of the most important stages in the development of each 'doctored' garden was the first meeting with the garden owners during the winter. It was then that the majority of the information needed to design the garden was assimilated. It was very important to draw out the desires and preferences of the owners, how they saw the space, what they had already decided about the function of the garden and how they saw it developing in the future.

Measurements and important details were established such as viewpoints, levels, overhanging trees; a compass reading was taken, then a set of photographs for reference. The owners were asked to draw up a list of likes and dislikes, specific things they wanted to include and exclude, and were also encouraged to gather together images from magazines and books to help formulate their ideal. At the end of the first meeting the basic concept for the garden was in place. The design of the garden was then developed back on the drawing board.

On our return visit the following spring the plan was instigated. Any last-minute adjustments were made to the design before the three days of construction and planting began. At the end of this stage, the re-landscaped garden was in place and the owners were briefed about a maintenance schedule to implement for the garden until we returned in the summer to check on progress and to advise on the development of the garden.

▶ *Just three months after planting and the Cotswolds garden looks established.*

Andy and Louise

A Family Garden
Cotswolds

The Client

The occupants of this semi-detached, stone-built house are Andy and Louise and their two small children, Rebecca who is at primary school and Jake who is just pre-school age. Andy designs and makes pots, garden ornaments and figures in terracotta for the nearby Whichford Pottery. As they had only recently moved into the house, they were still feeling their way into their new surroundings, both indoors and out, when we initially visited them.

They had inherited a garden which had, in its day, been very well laid out and carefully tended. Over recent years the previous occupant had struggled valiantly to keep the garden in order, but had gradually lost out to the encroaching weeds, so that a major overhaul was now needed. Like the house, the garden had also undergone a change of circumstances in that both now needed to meet the requirements of a young family rather than those of a single elderly householder.

Louise was already a budding gardener, and was keen to start on the new garden. Although Andy was less keen as a gardener he was thoroughly supportive of Louise and was eager to see his terracotta pots being used to their full potential. With two young children and the purchase of their first home, they did not have much to spend on making the garden, but despite this they did not seem daunted by the

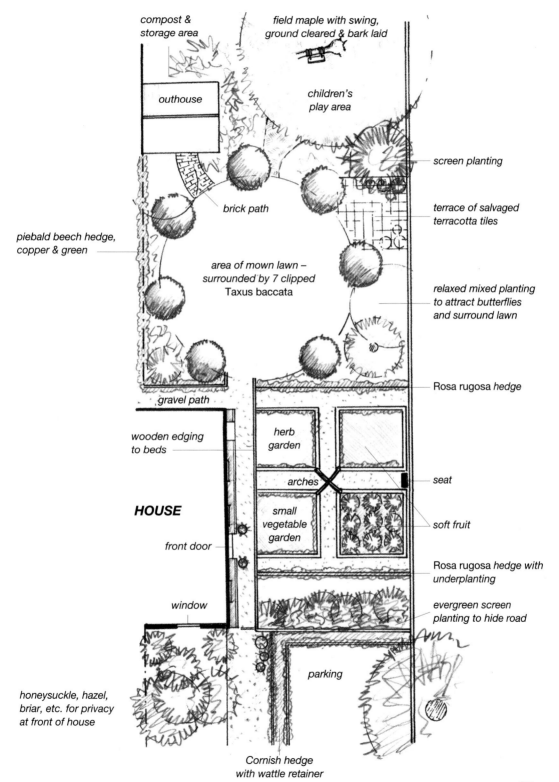

compost &
storage area

field maple with swing,
ground cleared & bark laid

outhouse

children's
play area

screen planting

brick path

terrace of salvaged
terracotta tiles

piebald beech hedge,
copper & green

area of mown lawn –
surrounded by 7 clipped
Taxus baccata

relaxed mixed planting
to attract butterflies
and surround lawn

Rosa rugosa *hedge*

gravel path

wooden edging
to beds

herb
garden

arches

seat

HOUSE

small
vegetable
garden

soft fruit

front door

Rosa rugosa *hedge with
underplanting*

window

evergreen screen
planting to hide road

honeysuckle, hazel,
briar, etc. for privacy
at front of house

parking

Cornish hedge
with wattle retainer

prospect, and both were excited by its potential.

Their main concern was the close proximity of the A44 trunk road, which ran directly alongside the property. They were anxious to screen the garden from the road, both for the children's safety and to reduce the noise of the traffic. They were also keen for the car parking area to be kept separate from the main garden – at present an overgrown asphalt drive ran the whole length of the garden to a parking space and they wanted this removed. They wanted to gain more space by removing the corrugated-iron garage that butted up to the stone outhouse which would ultimately become Andy's pottery, and had plans to develop the area underneath the old field maple at the end of the garden into a play area for the children.

Louise already had some definite ideas. She felt that there was no design to the garden at present and that it could be reorganized. The plants were a random mix of soft fruit, odd shrubs and overgrown perennials; Louise also thought that the two apple trees were good but in the wrong place, and that many perennials such as lupins, daisies and aquilegias could be re-used. She wanted the prostrate conifers, the dilapidated *Lonicera nitida* hedge and the weeping cherry to be removed.

▼ *Andy, Louise and their children in the family garden in the Cotswolds.*

Louise was an eclectic gardener, collecting cuttings from friends and bargains from plant fairs, and wanted a style that would suit her, relaxed and informal. She wanted an area for vegetables, herbs, soft fruit and top fruit, to provide food for as long a period as possible, in the narrowest section of the garden alongside the house, and expressed an interest in dividing the garden into distinct areas. A lawn was essential for the children, and storage for Andy's terracotta pots and nightlight-holders.

Before we left Andy and Louise showed us some innovative garden furniture a friend had constructed from salvaged wood, and pointed us in the direction of the Rollright standing stones, an ancient site nearby which they were particularly interested in, as a possible source of inspiration.

The Diagnosis

The garden wrapped around the end-of-terrace cottage forming an L-shape (if the area outside the living-room window is excluded) measuring 30m in length, 13m at its widest point and 10m at its narrowest, with railings and a strip of privet hedge separating the road from the garden. A sound drystone wall 1m (3ft) high separated the property from the village school next door, and an old lonicera hedge formed a boundary on the other side. Right of access to their garden had to be retained for the neighbours in the adjoining property. The old asphalt drive that at present divided the garden ran down its full length to a dilapidated garage at the end.

The garden faced south and was not overshadowed by any overhanging trees or neighbouring buildings. In fact the gable end of the school and the stone walls provided a pleasant backdrop. An old yew in the school grounds provided a solid evergreen foil at the road end, and a large ivy-

covered field maple gave some dappled shade and secrecy at the end of the garden, where there was also potential room for a greenhouse. The garden had obviously been well looked after until two or three years previously. There did not seem to be any obvious perennial weed problem and the soil was a light friable loam, though somewhat impoverished.

The screening of the main road took priority. Next came the division of the garden into areas: there would be an area for fruit, vegetables and herbs (the potager), a lawn with an area for shrubs and perennials, and a terrace alongside the wall to catch the sun. The wild area at the end of the garden was ideal as a play area for the children.

Once the garden was mapped out on paper it became clear that there were obvious ways to

▶ *The circular lawn creates an illusion of extra space.*

▼ *The potager consists of four beds of fruit and vegetables linked by an arch of hazel twigs.*

separate one area from the next. The small front garden leading from the road to the house was divided off first. The left-hand lawn would become a small wildflower sanctuary, planted with native shrubs – sweetbriar roses for their welcoming scent, and hazel to screen the road from the living-room window and blend with the hedgerows in the surrounding countryside. The right-hand side, with its privet hedge, would be sacrificed to accommodate offstreet parking for two cars. This area would be put down to gravel and softened with a mix of ox-eye daisies and poppies.

To separate the road and parking area from the garden, a 'Cornish hedge', an imitation of the planted banks in the West Country, would be placed level with the end of the house. The density of the wall would act as both a physical barrier and a screen. A 2m (6ft) high wattle door alongside the house provided access to the main garden, and the narrow section of the L-shape would be ideal for the potager. First, it was within easy reach of the kitchen, and second, it was enclosed by the Cornish hedge at one end and the house and boundary walls on either side. It would be divided into four 3m (10ft) square beds which would be edged with wood and separated by 1m (3ft) wide paths of pink crushed gravel to tie in with the local stone. The four beds would be linked with an arch made from hazel twigs, as a support for runner beans, climbing gourds and nasturtiums. The two beds alongside the wall would be planted with mixed soft and cordon fruit to screen the school, and the remaining beds would be devoted to a mix of herbs and vegetables. A *Rosa rugosa* hedge would run along the shrubbery at the base of the wall and also along the garden end to separate the main garden from the potager.

Andy and Louise's suggestion to visit the Rollright standing stones, an ancient site where the stones

form a circle around a central grass area, provided the inspiration for the main area of the garden. It was felt that the essence of this sacred site could be brought to the garden by providing a central circular lawn with seven surrounding yews, which would symbolize the stone circle. The simplicity of the circle would immediately provide a focal point in the garden as well as an expansive play lawn, and the yews, when they were established, would provide substance and presence the year round. Being at the lower end of the garden added to its safety aspect, as it encouraged the children to spend their time in an area well away from the road where they could also be easily observed from the kitchen. The remaining beds would be spacious enough for Louise's ever-increasing collection of plants and they would form a floral, informal enclosure directly in contrast to the formality of the layout of the potager. It was felt that a bold, simple layout would suit the family and enable them to add detail as they progressed.

Andy was keen to make a small enclosed terrace at the base of the sunny wall, to be constructed from handthrown tiles. The wall would be an ideal support for a vine and a storage place for his terracotta nightlight-holders. A simple brick path would lead to the pottery, and a bark path would lead through into the children's play area underneath the field maple.

The old lonicera hedge would be replaced with a piebald hedge of copper and green beech, which would retain its foliage in winter and in summer would create a foil for the border in front. Climbers such as the vigorous *Clematis* 'Bill Mackenzie' and rambling roses were placed along the walls to screen and smother the periphery of the garden and soften and blur the boundaries.

Because of lack of time and the fact that it was the wrong time of year, we were unable to complete the development work in the front garden. Ultimately, the plan is to strip the turf from this area and then re-sow it with a woodland mix of wildflowers. The entrance-way will be covered with rolled gravel, which will also be used for all of the paths in the centre section.

We did actually make a slight change to one of the central beds, to make sure that an inspection cover was positioned in a pathway rather than partly in a path and partly in one of the vegetable beds.

Hard Landscaping

This project began by clearing the garden of all plants worth saving; any which did not fit into the new scheme but were too good to throw away were distributed among friends and neighbours by Louise.

The heavy work started when the excavator moved in to break up the asphalt drive. Prior to this, we had measured and marked out the dimensions of the main path through the garden, as we did not want to dig up the drive and re-lay half of it again, as path, in exactly the same spot.

Next came the removal of two well-established trees which were very close to one another, an apple and an ornamental cherry. The original intention had been to save the apple and relocate it, but its root system was found to be in very poor condition, so we discarded it. We had never intended to keep the cherry tree, and this was dispatched to the skip. Another large apple tree was to be kept, and we used the excavator to move it further down the garden.

A well-established privet hedge along the road frontage of the property was dug up, and we discovered a section of wrought-iron railings along this front boundary. These were removed, and the soil level was reduced by 30cm (1ft) for a distance of 4m (12ft) into the garden to create the off-road parking area. We had to be very careful in this area as there

were obstacles: one was an inspection point for a foul drain, the other a telegraph pole on the very edge of the garden. After we had changed the soil level, we removed the top of the inspection pit and lowered the level by three courses of bricks (having already gained permission). This brought the top cover of this pit level with the surrounding area of the car park, and finally the top section was cemented back into position.

After the garden had been cleared and the soil turned using a rotovator, the separate areas of the new garden were marked so that the development work could begin in earnest. The first feature we concentrated on was the Cornish hedge. Support posts were driven into place, positioned to form a

---

Materials and equipment

Softwood stakes (3in x 2in x 6ft) tannalized
Wood for pegs (2in x 2in x 4m)
Softwood stakes (3in x 2in x 8ft) tannalized
Reinforcing rod (4 x 3m)
12mm plywood (1.2m x 2.4m x 9)
Wooden edging (6in x 1in x 84m)
Wire (25m)
Hazel sticks (4 bundles)
Wattle panels (12)
Wattle gate
Pink gravel (5cu m)
Mulch 'N' Mix (14 x 80 litres)
Rotovator
JCB excavator
Vibrating plate
2 Large rubbish skips
Sledgehammers
Chainsaw + full safety equipment
Heavy-duty electric hammer-drill
Rolawn heavy-duty turf-laying barrow

*(All measurements for the materials and equipment lists have been retained as a mixture of metric and imperial, as this is how these materials are commonly sized when bought from suppliers.)

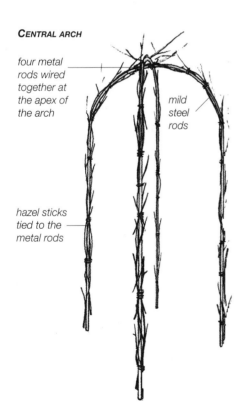

CENTRAL ARCH

four metal rods wired together at the apex of the arch

mild steel rods

hazel sticks tied to the metal rods

narrow alley 60cm (2ft) in width, to hold the wattle hurdles in position. In order to prevent soil spilling out through the gaps in the weave of the hurdles, the inside of the alley was lined with thick plywood. We were meticulous about firming each layer of soil we added in order to reduce the risk of settlement after the planting had been finished. Most of the soil for this earth bank was quite close at hand, being the surplus removed from the off-road parking area.

The middle section of the garden was directly opposite the house and consisted of four rectangular beds, linked in the centre by an arch of hazel twigs with an upright supporting leg positioned in each bed. The main strengthening of the structure was provided by four mild-steel rods incorporated into the arch and disguised by the hazel twigs. As the garden matures and the plants establish, climbers will grow over the structure to form a living arch linking the plants and the four sub-sections of the garden together.

These four garden beds were all raised above the surrounding paths by about 10cm (4in), and each one had a wooden retaining board around it to keep the

▶ *The rustic arch of hazel twigs supports runner beans, climbing gourds and nasturtiums.*

◀ *(Top) A view through the potager to the circular lawn beyond.*

▼ *The wattle hurdles retaining the Cornish hedge: this feature was used to separate the road and the parking area from the garden.*

border soil in place. The pathways were all made with a firmed sub-base and then covered with gravel, which is watered and compacted.

Soft Landscaping

Andy and Louise's garden provided several opportunities to create very different moods and growing areas. By setting the Cornish hedge back into the plot from the road, the front lawn was left on the 'outside' of the garden proper. To screen the living-room from the road we decided to leave this area as a wildflower patch to blend with the surrounding countryside. Woodland wildflowers were added to the existing turf, and on the road side of the patch we planted clumps of sweetbriar for its welcoming scented leaves and colourful hips, and hazel for its delicate growth. Wild honeysuckle was introduced to give scent and continuity with the surrounding hedgerows.

The Cornish hedge was planted with a mix of native plants to provide a visual and physical barrier from the road. Sweetbriar and hawthorn were used for their impenetrable growth and bird-attracting berries, with dogwood for its good autumn colour and its ability to fill out the lower skirts of the hedge. The gravel area put down for the path and parking area was sown directly with native poppy and ox-eye daisy seed to soften the entrance and make it appear as if it had been there for some time.

The garden side of the Cornish hedge was planted with a border to evergreens: *Viburnum rhytidophyllum* for its large noise-deflecting leaves and holly to screen the road still further. It was underplanted with doronicum and aquilegias salvaged from the garden. The *Rosa rugosa* hedge that separated this border from the potager ran the width of the garden. The hedge was selected for its dense growth, good

foliage, flowers and hips and also for the fact that it would not need pruning. To keep down weeds the hedge was underplanted with a carpet of shade- and drought-tolerant sweet woodruff.

A lavender hedge interplanted with hollyhocks was planted along the house to soften the exterior and provide year-round foliage. The potager, which was easy to reach from the kitchen, provided Louise with herbs, vegetables and fruit. We put herbs and rhubarb in the bed nearest the kitchen door and soft fruit in the furthest beds. Cordon fruit trees were planted along the back wall so they would ultimately increase the privacy from the school and provide a backdrop for this area of the garden. Wild strawberries were planted around the edges of the beds to soften the hard lines.

The hazel arch uniting the four beds of the potager and echoing the gable end of the school was planted with a riot of ornamental climbing gourds, sweet peas and nasturtiums to provide a focal point. Louise was encouraged to match leaf forms and textures in the potager so that this area of the garden felt full and burgeoning as you opened the garden gate. After we left she planted a golden hop to scramble through the wattle fence, and 'New Dawn' roses, honeysuckle and alpine clematis around the doors.

The main area of the garden was divided off from the potager by a matching *Rosa rugosa* hedge, and one of the apple trees was moved down to free up the potager. The central area of the garden, a large circular lawn with seven yews, had been inspired by our trip to see the ancient Rollright Stones. The yews connected with the yew in the school next door, 'borrowing' it and making it appear part of the garden. Eventually the 'standing' yews would provide powerful forms which would read as a simple contrast to the more frothy perennials in summer and as a strong structure for winter interest with long shadows and atmosphere in frosty weather.

When the lawn was made, we used large rolls of turf which could be laid just like a carpet, using a special trolley designed by the turf producer. We started by raking the area level and removing any large stones we found, and then raking the area over again in the opposite direction. To mark out the area, we found the central point and then scribed out a circle 30cm (1ft) larger than the intended size of the lawn. The rolls of turf were laid and firmed gently, then the central point of the lawn was re-located and a circle scribed to the exact size of the lawn. Finally, the turf was cut along this line with a 'half-moon' turf-cutter to provide a good firm edge to the grass.

The beds were left for Louise to plant with her eclectic mix of perennials and shrubs, a bold and relaxed look not tied down to specific colour schemes; she wanted the garden to be a home for learning and improvisation. The old scruffy *Lonicera nitida* hedge was replanted with the new piebald mixed hedge of copper and green beech, which would form a more interesting backdrop and hold its leaves in the winter.

Finally, to soften the buildings and the walls, we planted vigorous self-maintaining climbers such as the rambling rose 'Wedding Day' and *Clematis* 'Bill Mackenzie'. Both would be allowed to romp, thus giving the garden a less definable boundary.

Before we left we gave Louise a list of suggestions for plants including *Rosa moyesii* for its hips, and lavatera for long summer blooming. Andy wanted to plant a vine on the wall and use his terracotta pots, which Louise was keen to plant up. This was the point at which we felt it would be good to leave them to develop on their own. The bones were there, and they were ready to continue with developing the ideas they had begun to formulate for their new garden.

All the plants were chosen for their hardiness and for an appropriate sense of place. The planting would feel like a relaxed cottage garden, with elements such as the Cornish hedge to tie in with the landscape. And a strong bone structure installed at this stage would allow Louise to overlay any amount of detail.

Plants and seeds

Clematis 'Frances Rivis'
Clematis 'Markham's Pink'
Cornus sanguinea
Corylus avellana
Crataegus monogyna
Euonymus europaeus
Fagus sylvatica
Fagus sylvatica 'Atropurpurea'
Rosa moyesii
Rosa rugosa
Rosa 'New Dawn'
Rosa 'Wedding Day'
Rosmarinus officinalis
Taxus baccata
Viburnum rhytidophyllum

Apple tree (cordon)
Blackcurrants
Gooseberries
Loganberry
Pear tree 'Concorde' (cordon)
Raspberries
Rhubarb 'Timperley Early'

Beans (runner)
Gourds
Hollyhocks
Eau-de-cologne mint
Apple mint
Spearmint

SEEDS
Evening primrose
Ox-eye daisy
Poppy
Woodland flowers

Robin

A Long, Narrow Garden
Balham, London

▲ *Brad, Dan and Robin discuss the growth and maintenance of the plants in the Balham garden.*

The Client

This relatively small, narrow garden in suburban south London is owned by Robin, an actor. He is single, and describes himself as someone who is not by nature a townie and therefore greatly values access to an outside space in which to relax. He works irregular hours, and often finds himself with periods of free time, though he might also be away for several weeks at a time filming on location, so to some degree the garden would need to look after itself.

Regular garden maintenance, therefore, was not possible, but after a hectic filming schedule Robin feels he needs relaxation in natural surroundings, and simply putting the area down to a hard surface was out of the question. The garden was small enough for him to feel committed to completely rebuilding it from scratch. He was quite clear about what he wanted in the garden and how he saw himself using the space. He loathed what he had inherited from the previous owner – a small strip of lawn, a conifer and an oversized concrete pond made from what he described as rubbish pulled out of skips. He wanted a new start.

Robin provided us with an extensive list of likes and dislikes. He hated municipal bedding and preferred architectural foliage and plants which gave a feeling of the wild. He also compiled a board of magazine clippings which encapsulated what he wanted the garden to be – he had picked out images such as foxgloves growing through alchemilla and images of plants with bold and striking foliage such as bamboo and cardoons. He had singled out specific plants such as eucalyptus which he was keen to include, and the only plant already in the garden which he wanted to keep was the shiny-leaved acanthus.

Although Robin was fully aware of the limitations of the small space, he did make it quite clear that what he sought was a degree of privacy and a relaxed atmosphere in which he could potter and enjoy being outside. He was anxious that the view from his bedroom should be improved, and thought that the dingy alley could easily be enlivened with pots. He was quite pragmatic about parting with the lawn and felt that the space was really far too small to accommodate one. He wanted his garden to be burgeoning with rich colour, textures and foliage and a feel of the wild, a contrast to the surrounding suburbia.

The Diagnosis

This garden, which lay on the south side of a terraced row of houses, had previously been twice the site that it is today. The house had been divided into two flats, with the garden split into two by low larchlap fencing. There was an alley running alongside the kitchen extension which measured 1.5m x 8m and the main body of the garden measured 4m x 20m. Access to the garden from the house was from the side door of the extension into the alley, and outside access was from a small gate at the end which led on to a narrow alley running behind the gardens.

In terms of maintenance, the garden itself had been well looked after by its previous occupants. The alley was put down mostly to concrete, with a small border containing an acanthus and a winter-flowering

▲ *Laying bricks and decking across the main axis of this narrow garden gives an illusion of width.*

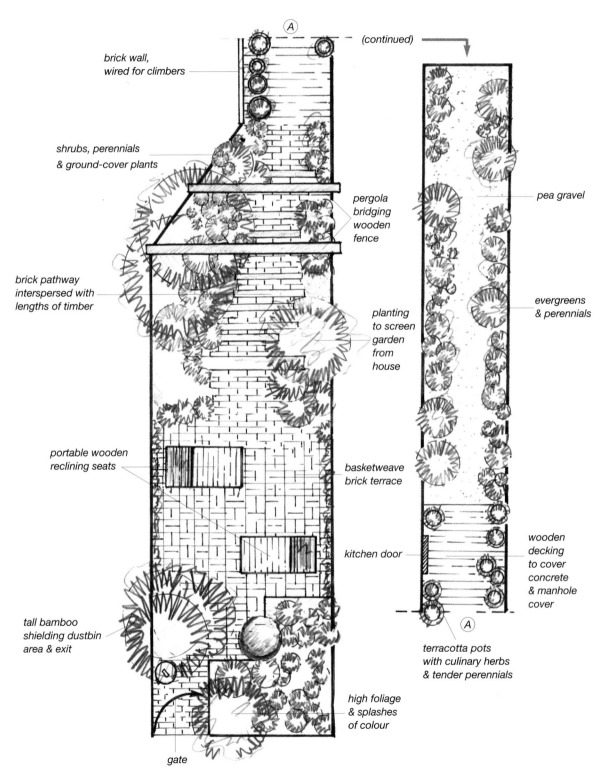

brick wall,
wired for climbers

shrubs, perennials
& ground-cover plants

pergola
bridging
wooden
fence

brick pathway
interspersed with
lengths of timber

planting
to screen
garden
from
house

portable wooden
reclining seats

basketweave
brick terrace

kitchen door

tall bamboo
shielding dustbin
area & exit

high foliage
& splashes
of colour

gate

(continued)

pea gravel

evergreens
& perennials

wooden
decking
to cover
concrete
& manhole
cover

terracotta pots
with culinary herbs
& tender perennials

A

jasmine running alongside the fence. The garden was dominated by a raised pool which was crude and entirely out of scale, and an oversized conifer shaded and overpowered the small space. A poorly lawn covered the rest of the area.

Good points were that there were no trees overshadowing the garden or invading the soil space with roots, and the sun fell on the garden for most of the day, until mid-afternoon. There were no changes in level, and the free-draining loam looked as if it would be a good growing medium if it was improved with organic matter.

Problems arose with access to the garden, and as with many town properties all the materials had to be trundled along the narrow alley at the back. We calculated that the best approach was to start close to the house and clear everything out by taking it down the garden towards the rear entrance. This enabled us to create a one-way flow, with new materials coming into the top of the garden as soon as it had been cleared. It also made the most effective use of our available labour, in what was a relatively small space. We could work in small teams, performing specific tasks, but minimize the problems of getting in one another's way.

The main aim was to try to achieve a greater feeling of space. Robin was anxious that the garden should have defined areas which would provide maximum interest over the year, and that it should have a certain amount of seclusion.

The plan was to divide the garden into three very distinct sections, giving the impression of a series of small individual gardens used for specific purposes while still retaining a link between them.

First, we decided to make a decent seating area, which would become the centre of the garden. To tie in with the brick of the buildings and wood of the fences the plan was to stick with these two materials for the hard landscaping. There would be a square terrace, the width of the garden, in the centre, with the other two sections providing a shield of planting to enclose the space and give it some sense of seclusion. Access to this terrace would be provided by a staggered brick path down from the kitchen door at the bottom of the alley. A dog-leg path up from the garden exit would distract the eye from the gate at the end.

To separate the alley from the main body of the garden, a simple double pergola would be erected at the end to frame the view of the garden and to give it a defined entrance, and this division would be further emphasized by a change of levels in the form of a single step down into the main garden, through the pergola. To give the impression that the garden was wider than it was, the mustard-yellow brickwork (recycled London stocks) would be inlaid with wood to echo the arbour above and provide a crossways reference.

The alley needed to be kept relatively free for access to the windows, so the first design set down slabs laid into gravel into which a green corridor of foliage would be planted. In the summer months, the alley is brightly lit and often very hot during the middle part of the day, then plunged into deep shade from mid-afternoon. In the winter, however, hardly any sunlight reaches this area of the garden. In an attempt to compensate for this problem, most of the plants in this area were to be grown in containers, allowing the plants to be moved and rearranged when necessary and re-sited in areas where the light is better.

Immediately outside the kitchen door, where the concrete paving could not be lifted, a wooden deck, with the slats again running widthwise, would provide

an area for large terracotta pots and gave a change in texture between the brick path and the gravel alley. This area tended to be very hot, and the pots would give an instant Mediterranean effect.

To provide some light screening on the brick terrace a light wood and wire trellis, with bamboo canes fastened to the wires, would be built on top of the fence and planted with the lacy white potato vine to partially screen out the neighbours. This would give one the impression of being in a private area that was not directly overlooked, although the advantage of this light screen was that it would not block out as much light as fencing would have done. The planting on either side of the path leading to the terrace would be a soft mix of shrubs and perennials designed to create a veil of foliage through which the rest of the

▲ *Dense planting smothers weeds and softens the edges of the hard landscaping.*

garden could be glimpsed. Three silver-stemmed eucalyptus would give privacy.

At the bottom of the garden, a box sphere on the corner would distract the eye from the path leading to the gate at the bottom of the garden. Vibrant red crocosmia would join the ever-moving zebra grass and rusty red day-lilies, and a black-stemmed bamboo, underplanted with red hot pokers, would give height and year-round colour, screen the dustbins, and provide a constant rustle of foliage. Finally a strawberry tree planted by the exit would give an evergreen backdrop and a welcome crop of orange fruits in the winter.

Hard Landscaping

The bulk of the initial work involved clearing and levelling the site, including breaking up and removing the old pond. In order to speed up this operation and improve the working conditions, Robin had drained the pool several weeks earlier, and it was dry when we arrived. The task luckily turned out to be easier than anticipated, as the bulk of the pond's structure was above soil level; this made the operation of dismantling it much easier (by hand with lump hammers and chisels, and by electric-powered hammer-drill on the more substantial parts of the structure) and eliminated the need to fill a large hole with rubble and soil to re-adjust the level. A section of pathway running alongside the house also had to be broken up, in order to provide the maximum growing area in the garden.

The large conifer which dominated the garden was removed by digging a trench around the rootball, tying a rope close to the top of the stem and a team of helpers pulling for all they were worth. We had deliberately left the top on this plant so that we could use its height as a lever, making pulling it over very much easier. A number of plants were saved which did not fit into the scheme but were too good to be thrown away, and Robin distributed these among his friends and neighbours.

Once everything had been removed from the site, we proceeded to level it. A rough level-over and single digging began the process of creating the new garden. We all walked over the site to firm it, and finally the whole area was raked level and firmed again. Once we reached this stage, matters began to proceed at a brisk pace, helped by the enthusiasm of staff and students from the Berkshire College of Agriculture.

The bulk of the hard landscaping and construction work consisted of laying the brick paving. Although the pattern and arrangement of the bricks would vary depending on which section of the garden we were working in, the basic preparation was the same for all areas. The paving was to be of a 'flexible' nature – a technique where no mortar is used and the bricks or blocks are laid on a bed of dry sand. One advantage of this system is that the paving can easily be lifted and re-laid if required. We started by thoroughly compacting the base of the area to be paved, using a petrol-driven vibrating plate to firm and settle the soil. Next a 2.5cm (1in) layer of dry loose sand was spread evenly over the area to 'bed' the bricks on to. The bricks were then packed tightly on to the sand, and locked into position by brushing fine dry sand between them.

The pathway in the middle of the garden was intended to give an appearance of greater width, and consisted of bricks laid across the longitudinal axis of the garden on their edge, to make them look narrower, in a 'stretcher bond' arrangement. Strips of wood incorporated among the bricks further emphasized the width. The path was laid in a gentle curve through the garden, giving a sense of flow and movement.

In the end section of the garden, the brick paving was laid in a basketweave pattern, to give the seating area a square feel and appearance. This has the effect of restricting the impression of movement and creating a feeling of having arrived within a key area of the garden.

The two arches forming the pergola consisted of two sections of 10 x 5cm (4 x 2in) timber supported horizontally at 2.4m (8ft) above the path; 40mm (1½in) copper tube, concreted into the ground immediately adjacent to the path, formed the upright supports. Deep holes were dug here, with at least 30cm (1ft) of

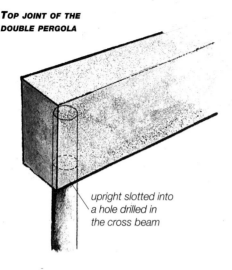

**TOP JOINT OF THE
DOUBLE PERGOLA**

*upright slotted into
a hole drilled in
the cross beam*

Materials and equipment

Bamboo canes (1m/3ft)
Bricks (London stocks)
Terracotta pots (various sizes)
Steel upright posts
Copper piping (40mm/1½in)
Wood stain (exterior 'Dark Blue')
Timber (tannalized 4in x 2in/10cm x 5cm)
Wooden recliners
Sharp sand (1cu m)
Slow-release fertilizer
Growmore general-purpose fertilizer
Mulching material (14 x 80 litres)
Vibrating plate (for compacting sand
    bed and paving)
Heavy-duty electric hammer-drill
    (for breaking up the pond)
Rubbish skips (2)

---

topsoil over the concrete fixing, the idea being to leave a sufficient depth of soil to enable us to plant climbers close to the base of each upright and train them up over the archway we had created.

In the end section of the garden, which was intended to be the main seating area, we attached wooden posts to the existing fence, which extended to a height of 2 metres (6ft). Four strips of thin wire were strung between these posts, and 1 metre (3ft) bamboo canes were suspended vertically from these wires at 5cm (2in) intervals.

Finally we built the wooden deck outside the back door, to cover the concrete we could not move. In fact, because this was placed directly on to the concrete rather than being raised, it was a 'duckboard' rather than a deck. We built this at the very end of the final day, when most of the other projects had been finished and the amount of foot traffic into and out of the house was down to an absolute minimum.

Soft Landscaping

Robin's garden was divided into two distinct sections: an alley which, although shady in the winter, caught the afternoon sunshine in the summer, and the main body of the garden which was basically bright and sunny, neither overhung by trees nor undermined by neighbouring roots. He wanted a garden which was full of interest throughout the year, and he was particularly keen on bold architectural foliage and rich saturated colour. In a garden as small as this, though, careful plant selection was paramount.

The alley was the first area that Robin saw in the morning from his bedroom window, and he wanted it to be green and welcoming. It was randomly planted with a mixture of evergreen perennials, using ground cover such as the shade-tolerant epimediums with silver spikes of astelia as vertical contrast. Herbaceous perennials such as spring-flowering pulmonarias were chosen for seasonal interest of leaf and flower, with ferns and tall spears of the bronze-leaved cimicifuga for their soft fresh growth. The cimicifugas in particular would create a partial screen in the summer and add height. The glossy-leaved acanthus that Robin liked was retained for its light-reflecting foliage, and the fences were left unclothed to prevent the alley from seeming any more narrow. The look was designed for its layers of interest, like a green tapestry.

Beyond the wooden decking, with its terracotta pots, a semi-evergreen honeysuckle was planted to soften the party wall and give scent around the door. Dark *Clematis* 'Rouge Cardinal' was planted to lace over the arch and provide a significant entrance to the garden from the kitchen door.

The first borders on either side of the path were planted with delicate wiry plants such as Spanish broom, for its scent and summer splash of gold, and the elegant *Verbena bonariensis*. This theme was continued with tall oat grasses, *Stipa gigantea*, to soar to 2m (6ft) and provide a tactile and ever-shifting partial screen to the garden beyond. Clouds of bronze fennel interplanted with brown foxgloves and inky-purple buddlejas added body without making the planting heavy. For height and winter interest we planted three young eucalyptus trees together; they would ultimately form a multi-stemmed small tree which would give partial privacy.

The paths were softened with purple sage and dark-leaved *Viola labradorica*, and fairy wing poppies were sown into the cracks. The terrace was left as uncluttered as possible. White potato vine, *Solanum jasminoides* 'Album', was planted on the screens on

either side, and eschscholzias were sown into the paving around the perimeter for brilliant splashes of colour and to soften the space with their delicate foliage.

In the bottom borders, divided by the dog-leg path, a black-stemmed bamboo in the angle, underplanted with red hot pokers, related to the evergreen eucalyptus at the top of the garden and the clipped box sphere directly opposite. The planting in the largest bottom border was rich and impenetrable – it would conceal the neighbouring gardens and form a vibrant background to the rest of the garden. Tall zebra-striped grasses interplanted with vivid scarlet crocosmia and rusty-red day-lilies were backed by large-leaved *Macleaya cordata*, with coral plumes in summer and silvered undersides to the leaves.

The soil in this garden was in a very sorry state, with little or no organic matter and very little worm activity. To help the new plants establish quickly, a generous amount of fertilizer and organic compost was dug into the existing soil to a full fork's depth. Mixing the soil and compost to this depth encourages the plants to root deeply. In a dry hot garden such as this one it is very important to promote deep rooting, as this gives the plants more resistance to drought. Almost all the plants were grown in containers, and we did not tease out the roots when we planted (which is sometimes recommended) as we wanted to minimize root disturbance.

A generous handful of general fertilizer was scattered around each plant when it was firmed into position, and each was given a good watering immediately after planting. One or two containers were quite dry when we came to plant them, and these were soaked in a bowl of water until the rootball was thoroughly wet.

After planting, a 5cm (2in) thick mulch of organic matter was applied over the soil to reduce water loss and prevent weed seeds germinating. The smaller plants were covered with large plant pots before we added the mulch, to prevent them being smothered, and these pots were then removed leaving the plants exposed and free from mulch and dirt on the leaves.

As soon as all the planting and mulching was finished, a water-sprinkler was used to soak the mulch and the soil beneath.

◀ **Cynara** (Cardoon)**, Foeniculum** (Fennel) **and Digitalis** (Foxglove)**.**

▶ **Miscanthus and Macleaya.**

Plants and seeds

Ajuga reptans
Alchemilla mollis
Allium schoenoprasum
Arbutus unedo
Astelia chathamica
Buddleja 'Black Knight'
Buxus sempervirens
Canna 'Black Knight'
Cimicifuga racemosa
   'Purpurea'
Clematis x jackmanii
Clematis 'Rouge Cardinal'
Convolvulus cneorum
Crocosmia masonorum
Cynara cardunculus
Diascia rigescens
Dianthus 'Sops in Wine'
Dierama pulcherrimum

Digitalis ferruginea
Dryopteris filix-mas
Epimedium x versicolor
Eschscholzia
Euphorbia characias
Euphorbia robbiae
Eucalyptus pauciflora
x Fatshedera lizei
Foeniculum vulgare
   'Purpureum'
Geranium sanguineum
Hemerocallis 'Stafford'
Kniphofia 'Prince Igor'
Lathyrus latifolius
Lavandula angustifolia
Lonicera japonica 'Repens'
Macleaya cordata
Miscanthus sinensis 'Zebrinus'

Papaver rhoeas
Phyllostachys nigra
Pulmonaria 'Sissinghurst
   White'
Rosa glauca
Rosmarinus officinalis
Salvia ambigens
Salvia officinalis
   'Purpurescens'
Spartium junceum
Solanum jasminoides 'Album'
Stachys byzantina
Stipa gigantea
Thymus x citriodorus
Tiarella cordifolia
Verbena bonariensis
Vitis vinifera 'Purpurea'
Viola labradorica

Camberwell

A Town Communal Garden
Camberwell, London

The Client

This garden, like many in London, is a well-kept secret. From the road outside, you get no indication that when you pass through the wrought-iron gate in one corner you will enter a small close of about twelve dwellings, with the garden as a centrepiece. The flats face one another across the garden, and there is a wall at each end, leaving a relatively small space to be shared by all the occupants. In many respects, the planning and construction of this garden development was very much a community project. The group ranged right across the demographic spectrum, from senior citizens to a toddler, and in their own way everyone became as involved in the garden as their time and commitments allowed.

The individual ideas that had come together as a collective concept were surprisingly homogenous, considering the numbers involved. Most of the group had bought their flats specifically because of the open yet secluded 'courtyard' space, which was an unusual feature in this area.

Early on in the first meeting it became clear that the existing concrete slab path was necessary for access to each flat, and should be retained; although the group were not happy with it as a surface, it was agreed that it could be improved with careful planting to spill over it from both sides. The other consideration was the central lawn which had been

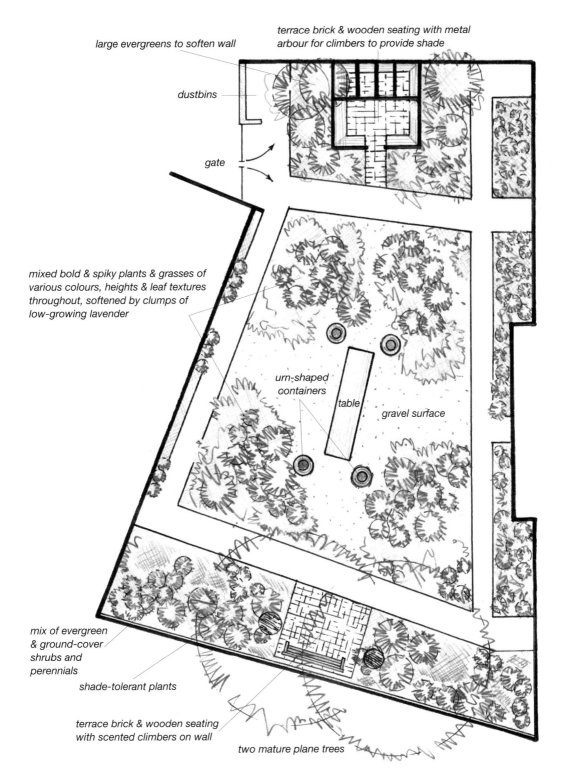

large evergreens to soften wall

terrace brick & wooden seating with metal arbour for climbers to provide shade

dustbins

gate

mixed bold & spiky plants & grasses of various colours, heights & leaf textures throughout, softened by clumps of low-growing lavender

urn-shaped containers

table

gravel surface

mix of evergreen & ground-cover shrubs and perennials

shade-tolerant plants

terrace brick & wooden seating with scented climbers on wall

two mature plane trees

▲ *Some of the residents at Camberwell enjoying the*
new surroundings of their communal garden.
▶ *The effect of colour is added to by sound, provided*
by wind rustling through ornamental grasses.

thrown down by the landscapers. We suggested to
the group that it would require a considerable
investment in maintenance terms and that it would be
better to remove it and plant instead. Almost without
exception they agreed.

Individual thoughts among the group were far-
ranging – a greenhouse and an orchard, for example.
Unanimously, though, it was agreed that the garden
should contain distinct areas – including a retreat in
the shade and somewhere to sit in sunshine. The
general feeling was that by definition the space was a
communal one and that there was nothing wrong with
it being shared, and it was decided that as long as
there were distinct areas within the garden it should
be left as one space, with no formal divisions.

In terms of planting everyone favoured a degree of
'organized chaos' and a look which felt relaxed. They
wanted masses of greenery and a garden which
would become their own urban oasis.

The Diagnosis

This was, above all, a communal garden, and to meet
the needs of all the group it had to be divided into
three distinct areas. The skill for the designer was to
ensure that each of the elements within the garden
appealed to the maximum number of residents.

Due to the wide range of ages, interests and
requirements among the group, this garden needed to
have a bit of everything: a sunny spot, with light shade
provided by plants; an area in deeper shade, because
parts of this garden could be very hot by mid-
afternoon in summer; plenty of seating areas, so that
the residents could have some privacy and not be
forced to sit together unless they chose to; a central
communal area with a large table and benches, for
those warm summer evenings when the group felt like
getting together.

The plants for this garden had to be those that
would require little care and attention, yet would provide
seasonal interest and tolerate hot dry conditions. The
advantage of gardening in London is that the city has a
microclimate all of its own, and is usually two or three
degrees warmer than the surrounding countryside. This
effect was further exaggerated by the enclosed position

of the garden, and meant that a greater range of plants, including some considered to be slightly tender, could be chosen.

In many respects, this project became a catalyst for drawing the residents together and developing a community spirit. Although the planning meetings were slow at the start, by the time we actually arrived to start implementing the design there was absolutely no stopping these people. Within an hour of starting in bright sunshine the weather turned foul, but by then it did not seem to matter. This garden had a momentum all of its own, and all of us were being carried along with it – even to the extent of clearing the old garden while snow was falling. However, this was the only day in the entire first series when our progress was disrupted by bad weather.

The only place in the garden where we were unable to follow the brief as closely as we would have liked was in some of the planting beneath the London plane trees. Due to their root spread, we were unable to plant as closely to the base of the trees as we would have liked. On the other hand, we had a pleasant surprise when we discovered that the floor in the arbour could be based on part of an old tarmacadam footpath at exactly the correct depth to form a sub-base for the brick paved area.

We encountered one problem almost from the start. We had originally planned to strip off the turf from the central lawn and stack it in one corner of the site, the intention being to use this valuable source of organic matter to make compost. Before we had removed half the turf we realized that we had far too much, and reluctantly we had to wheelbarrow it all in the opposite direction and throw it into a skip. This decision was realistic but largely unpopular, as it did seem rather wasteful.

During the operation of levelling the site to make

the central gravel paths, we came across a large concrete plinth buried in the middle of the garden area. Digging around this obstruction to determine its size, we realized that there was no possibility of removing it unless we hired some pretty substantial machinery. As usual, however, standing back and taking a look made all the difference, and we were able to come up with a workable compromise. The top 15cm (6in) was broken off the plinth so that it could be covered over with gravel, and the position of the table was moved by about 1m (3ft) so that it was sitting directly over the plinth.

We also had to deal with large amounts of rubbish left by some building contractors who had worked on the site previously. Not only did we have to dig up and remove this waste material, but we had to order an extra skip to have it taken away.

Hard Landscaping

The area to be developed was almost level, with only a slight fall across the site. Clearing the turf, a job which had to be done first, was not particularly taxing physically, but time was lost when it had to be moved a second time.

As soon as the site was clear, we used a rotary cultivator to dig over the central area. This task quickly became an archaeological exploration of twentieth-century artefacts. The previous year, a company of builders had been employed to renovate some of the flats, and we soon had a good idea of their feeding habits as we dug up soft drinks containers, polystyrene cartons advertising fast food chains and sandwich wrappers. In addition, we unearthed quantities of paving slabs, broken bricks, large pieces of wood, flattened oil-containers, and solid bags of cement. These discoveries went a long way towards explaining why the turf had been looking so awful.

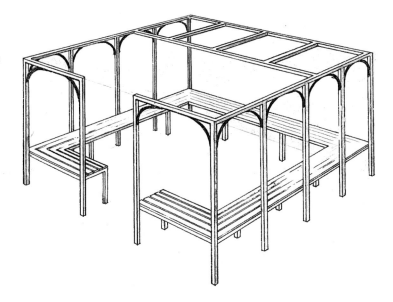

METAL ARBOUR

At the end of the garden closest to the entrance, a seating area was to be built. As soon as this part of the site had been cleared, we began setting out levels, marking out where the brick paved area would be positioned and digging out for the sub-base to be laid. While this work was going on, the metal arbour was being delivered in prefabricated sections. Once the sub-base had been prepared, the metal structure could be concreted into position and bolted into special fittings set in holes drilled into the wall to make it rigid. Finally, cross-pieces were welded on to the top to tie the entire arbour together.

The frame then had to be allowed to set into the concrete base before the brick flooring of the terrace could be laid, so the rest of the day was allowed for this. The following morning we began to lay the yellow London stock brick flooring. This was laid in a basketweave pattern on to a bed of dry sand, and once the bricks had been laid in place, they were fixed into position by brushing fine sand into the joints between them. The bricks were then firmed into the sand-bed with a vibrating plate. We laid a piece of old carpet over the bricks while we were using the vibrating plate, to prevent them getting chipped and marked by the metal of the plate.

While the concrete was setting, we made progress at the opposite end of the garden on the other brick

Materials and equipment

Yellow gravel (20 tonnes)
Organic mulch (7cu m)
Mulch 'N' Mix (10 x 80 litres)
Growmore (14kg)
Slow-release fertilizer (2kg)
Bricks (London stock)
Paving slabs (60cm x 60cm)
Metal arbour frame
Wooden benches and supports for arbour
Wood for table (2in x 9in x 56ft) tannalized
Wood for trestles
Wood for benches (2in x 9in x 28ft) tannalized
Carpenter for table/benches
Large pots (Thai, 28 x 4in)
Vibrating plate
Rotovator
Rubbish skips (2)
Sand for bedding brick (5cu m)

◀ Achillea *and* Stipa tenuissima.

▶ *The long banquet table and shady retreat in the distance.*

▼ *The arbour partially clothed in honeysuckle. Evergreen phormium and lavandula enclose the retreat.*

terrace, which was to provide a shaded retreat, with an open-slatted garden bench to be positioned between two mature plane trees. Once more we set out the levels, marked out the positions for the brick paved area, and dug out the soil for the sub-base to be laid and firmed. The brick flooring was laid in the same way as the first terrace.

In the central section of the garden, where the table would stand, the surface would be covered with gravel, as would all the pathways leading to it. The bulk of the hard landscaping here consisted of laying about 20 tonnes of yellow gravel to form a firm, all-weather surface. After levelling the central area to follow the slight natural slope of the site, we marked the boundaries of each pathway with pegs set at the required height. Bags of gravel were then brought into the garden on wheelbarrows and laid out at set intervals, before being split open and the gravel spread out. This was then firmed lightly with rakes and we all walked back and forth over it until the levels were right. The gravel was then thoroughly drenched with water and compacted again, but this

time using a vibrating plate to give a firm surface. The hardness of this surface is the result of the many different particle sizes of gravel being washed and settled by the water and then bound together when the pressure of the vibrating plate is applied.

Soft Landscaping

This communal garden presented the opportunity to create a green oasis in the inner city. The decision to remove the central lawn allowed us to rethink completely the hard confines and the aesthetics of the courtyard space.

The garden fell into three distinct areas. The centre would be put down to gravel, interplanted with a naturalistic mix of shrubs, perennials and grasses – this area would become the communal centre of the garden, with a giant table framed by four giant urns. The area underneath the trees would provide a shady retreat for the summer, and the sunny part of the garden at the base of the tall wall would make a scented area in the sunshine.

There would be unity of planting throughout the

garden so that the beds linked the whole area; relaxed, burgeoning growth would soften the paths and create a natural movement. Key evergreens would give the garden winter interest, and in the remaining seasons there would be surges of growth which would push through, one layer taking over from the next. The perennials were all long-lived varieties, and many, such as the sedum, achillea and fennel, were chosen for their interesting winter skeletons.

The central area was designed to be almost like a natural meadow, with a limited range of perennials planted in naturalistic drifts, one planting merging into the next. Repetition was vital, to maintain continuity throughout the area and prevent it looking like a traditional border. We started by introducing a framework of shrubs, *Buddleja* 'Lochinch' and *Phlomis fruticosa*, to provide partial screening of the table. These were softened with randomly planted *Cortaderia richardii*, a close relative of the pampas grass, with arching plumes that would add height and grace in midsummer. Once these key plants were placed, we planted *Achillea* 'Apricot Beauty' for its carpeting, ground-smothering growth and 60cm (2ft) tall heads of flowers which changed from brick-pink through to apricot and finally to cream as the season progressed. The horizontal flower heads continued with the autumn-flowering *Sedum* 'Autumn Joy', which provided bulk in the summer and butterfly food in the autumn. Both these plants, together with large clumps of billowing bronze fennel, provided interesting winter shapes.

In contrast to the horizontal forms, grasses were introduced to add to the meadow feeling and soften the look. Grasses are an excellent addition to a garden, providing a continual movement in the breeze. We used only clump-forming varieties: *Molinia caerulea* 'Moorhexe' for its 1.2m (4ft) vertical flowers and the shorter *Stipa tenuissima* for its soft gentle movement. We interplanted the grasses as if they had sown themselves, breaking up the drifts of perennials and merging with the shrubs.

The four large urns were planted with the architectural foliage of *Melianthus major*, which would add drama and act as a contrast to the soft planting surrounding them. The sides of the urns were softened with trailing dark purple *Surfinia petunias*. These could be replaced by winter bedding, for example blood-red wallflowers.

The small borders running the length of the buildings were planted with shade-tolerant *Viburnum davidii* for structure and interplanted with sweet woodruff as ground cover and *Acanthus mollis* for height and for its good glossy foliage, which in London starts into growth early. The sunny side of the border was planted with bloody cranesbill, which was linked in places into the central area and big billowing clumps of lavender.

The lavender was continued around into the planting surrounding the sunny retreat. It was broken up with the stray verticals of *Phormium tenax* and *Miscanthus sinensis* 'Gracillimus', which was also linked into the central area. A *Magnolia grandiflora* on one side of the arbour and *Arbutus x andrachnoides*, with its colourful bark, were planted to provide evergreen height, soften the walls and enclose the retreat. The retreat itself was planted with a repeat-flowering honeysuckle, *Lonicera periclymenum* 'Graham Thomas', and a white-flowered wisteria which would eventually clothe the wall. The walls of the buildings were left bare, to cut down on maintenance, although on our summer return visit the residents were already thinking about climbers and wall shrubs.

The shady retreat was softened by large clumps of

delicate bamboo, *Arundinaria nitida*, to provide a foil for the rest of the garden. The wall itself was planted with a mix of pale-leaved *Hedera helix* 'Buttercup', climbing hydrangea for its froth of white flowers and the blue *Clematis alpina* 'Frances Rivis' for early flower. The bamboos were interplanted with golden-leaved elder to give an impression of artificial sunlight in shade and a continuation of *Viburnum davidii* towards the front. The shrubs were broken up by big clumps of the delicate white *Aruncus dioicus* with a ground cover of evergreen *Euphorbia robbiae* and *Tellima grandiflora* for brilliant spring flowers. Vertical accents were supplied by occasional clumps of *Iris foetidissima*.

We mulched the whole garden quite heavily, because of the hot, dry conditions. To reduce moisture loss from the soil surface, using an organic mulch, a minimum layer of 5cm (2in) is adequate, but for suppressing weeds as well, a depth of 7.4–10cm (3–4in) is necessary. In the central area, a 2.5cm (1in) thick gravel mulch was applied immediately after planting. All the plants used in this garden were container-grown, but we still gave each one a good soaking as soon as it had been planted. We found that the most effective method of applying the water was to leave a hosepipe (with the water barely trickling) among the plants, and move it every half-hour. This way the water soaks down around the roots rather than evaporating from the soil surface. Sprinklers may look impressive but they do not give as good a result. The climbers which were planted against the arbour and up against the wall at the shaded end of the garden were tied into position immediately after planting to help prevent them being damaged, and allow them to establish quickly.

Plants and seeds

Acanthus latifolius
Acanthus mollis
Achillea 'Apricot Beauty'
Achillea 'Lachsschönheit'
Alchemilla mollis
Arbutus x *andrachnoides*
Aruncus dioicus
Arundinaria nitida
Buddleja 'Lochinch'
Calamagrostis x *acutiflora*
Clematis alpina 'Frances Rivis'
Cortaderia richardii
Euphorbia robbiae
x *Fatshedera lizei*
Foeniculum vulgare 'Purpureum'
Galium odoratum
Geranium macrorrhizum
Hedera helix 'Buttercup'
Hydrangea petiolaris
Iris foetidissima
Lavandula angustifolia
Lonicera periclymenum 'Graham Thomas'
Lonicera japonica 'Repens'
Magnolia grandiflora
Melianthus major
Molinia caerulea 'Moorhexe'
Miscanthus sinensis 'Gracillimus'
Phlomis fruticosa
Phormium tenax
Sambucus racemosa 'Plumosa Aurea'
Sedum 'Autumn Joy'
Stipa tenuissima
Surfinia petunias
Tellima grandiflora
Viburnum davidii
Wisteria floribunda 'Alba'

◀ **Acanthus latifolius** *growing through sweet woodruff.*

◀ *(Opposite)* **Lonicera 'Graham Thomas'** *climbing up a corner post of the arbour.*

▼ *Dense planting provides the definition of the garden.*

Kirsten and Isabelle

A Garden for Parent and Child
Norwich

The Client

The occupants of this council house on the outskirts of Norwich are Isabelle and her mother, Kirsten, who enjoy spending time in the garden when the weather is fine. Isabelle attends the local play-group several mornings a week, and Kirsten, who is unemployed, often spends time at the same centre working as a helper. Being a single parent, she looks after herself and Isabelle on a tight budget, and the garden came well down her list of priorities, but they both have an interest in plants, and Kirsten, being vegetarian, wanted to produce some of her own food if she could. She and Isabelle had grown carrots and sunflowers the previous year.

Kirsten was quite clear about the concept behind her garden, which she wanted to be as much for Isabelle as for adults. She was keen that the garden should not be formal and flat, and that an element of wilderness should be retained so that there would be a sense of risk and adventure to stimulate children. Although she didn't want any poisonous berries, she was anxious to retain plants like nettles and brambles which would remind Isabelle of the dangers often present in nature. She loved mysterious corners, pointing out a hole in the hedge which led to Isabelle's den.

With very little money and not a great deal of spare time, Kirsten was

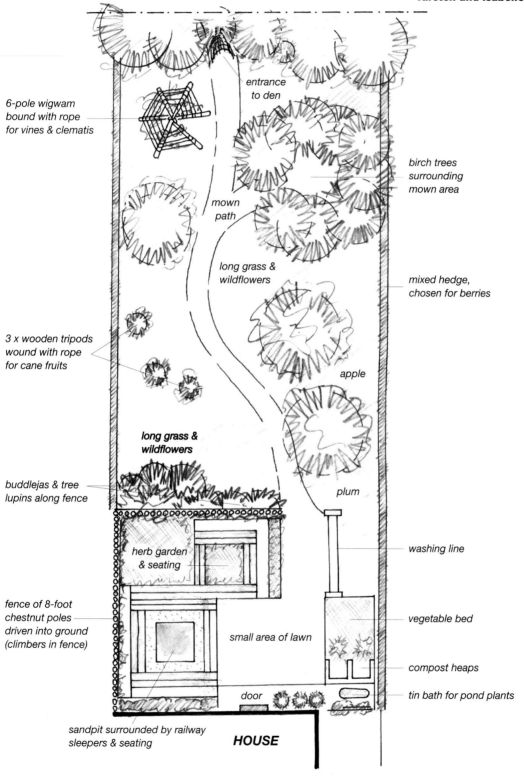

6-pole wigwam
bound with rope
for vines & clematis

entrance
to den

birch trees
surrounding
mown area

mown
path

long grass &
wildflowers

mixed hedge,
chosen for berries

3 x wooden tripods
wound with rope
for cane fruits

apple

long grass &
wildflowers

buddlejas & tree
lupins along fence

plum

washing line

herb garden
& seating

fence of 8-foot
chestnut poles
driven into ground
(climbers in fence)

vegetable bed

small area of lawn

compost heaps

door

tin bath for pond plants

sandpit surrounded by railway
sleepers & seating

HOUSE

◀ **Kirsten and the Garden Doctors view the transformation of her garden.**
▶ **Sunflowers in full bloom in the Norwich garden.**
▼ **The wigwam was constructed in the play area to provide a sense of adventure and stimulation for Kirsten's daughter, Isabelle.**

anxious that the garden should be low-maintenance and ecologically orientated so that materials were recycled. She did not want to use any pesticides. There was a large area of wild meadow which would reduce labour input and encourage wildlife into the garden. As part of the scheme she wanted a retreat for herself, a private den of her own with a spiritual feel to it that she could escape into; she also wanted an area nearer the house where she and Isabelle could grow herbs and vegetables.

Kirsten compiled a list of likes and dislikes – the likes included berry plants for birds, fruit trees, vegetables and a sandpit for Isabelle. She talked about decorating the sandpit with found stones and shells and creating a garden which would grow with the family.

The Diagnosis

The garden was overgrown with long coarse grass and had been invaded by wild brambles, which had gradually become established to the point of colonizing large areas of the garden. The remains of an old garage had become dangerous (particularly for a child), with coils of old half-rusted wire, rusting sections of jagged metal, glass fragments, rotting wood and broken asbestos, all partly covered with long grass, brambles and bindweed. Access to the rear garden was restricted by the presence of an old delivery van (minus a working engine) which was

located at the side of the house.

The site sloped quite steeply away from the house towards the bottom of the garden, where a large well-established privet hedge which had been left unpruned for a number of years now stood almost 3m (9ft) high. In the top section of the garden, about 4m (12ft) from the house, a large section of concrete slab had been laid, which was also partially overgrown, and a concrete path ran across the garden to join this slab.

This was the first garden of the series, and fortunately we were able to follow the brief quite closely. By the time we had finished we had covered all the points within the brief, and the result seemed to far exceed Kirsten's expectations. All the soft landscaping went ahead without a hitch, and the hard landscaping called for only relatively minor adjustments as we worked. The erection and construction of a wigwam structure (as part of Isabelle's play area) in the long-grass area ran like clockwork and, due to its shape and size, it became the dominant feature of the garden.

The section of the garden containing the derelict garage presented quite a problem, as this was the area chosen for the vegetable garden. The soil had to be carefully dug over and sifted to remove any remaining foreign bodies, such as small pieces of metal and glass – a lengthy process, but one which had to be done if the area was to be suitable for growing vegetables.

We had not intended to do a great deal of work on the privet hedge, and eventually decided to avoid pruning it at all. The main reason for this was that it was spring and many birds had already started to build nests within the hedge; it would scarcely have been fair to start off an ecologically friendly garden by evicting some of the residents.

The slope of Kirsten's garden proved to be much steeper than had originally been planned for, and this initially presented a problem for the hard landscape area at the top end of the garden. Consequently, we had two options available to us: either to build the hard-landscape feature into a series of split levels, working with the slope, or to change the topography of the site by importing vast quantities of infill material by hand, and completely removing the slope at the top end of the garden.

Hard Landscaping

Because of the dramatic changes planned for this garden, we felt we needed to start with a clean slate, to see exactly what we were dealing with, so all the unwanted material and debris had to be collected, wheelbarrowed around to the front of the house, and loaded into a skip to await collection.

The entire garden was cut with a strimmer to reduce the grass height, and the debris was cleared away along with the brambles and rubbish. The remains of the old garage and the various bits of wire, metal and glass were removed, and the soil was carefully dug over and sifted to remove any remaining small pieces.

As soon as the area close to the house had been cleared, we could start to set levels and mark out the positions for the sandpit and other features. Setting out and marking the work area is often a slow and laborious operation, but it is essential to get it absolutely correct before any excavation is started.

Two play areas were planned for this garden. The one in the top third was to consist of an enclosed area combined with a herb garden, seating area and sandpit. The seating consisted of reclaimed timber, with a fence of upright chestnut poles (resembling a stockade) providing a boundary to enclose the formal part of the garden.

The hard surface here was made from old railway sleepers; these are a safer surface for children than slabs or concrete, as there is less chance of serious injury when falling against them. By carefully arranging the interlocking areas on the three levels, it was possible to use the slope to best advantage. This was just one of the projects where the enthusiasm and skills of landscaping students from the nearby Norfolk College of Agriculture were fully utilized. Because of the size of the timber sections, particularly the railway sleepers, a chainsaw was used for cutting the wood.

The second play area, in the long-grass section of the garden, consisted of the large wigwam structure; this was wound with strong durable rope, enabling it to be used as a climbing frame and to provide support for climbing vines and clematis. Close by, under the existing privet hedge, a partially hidden den made of wicker was placed for Isabelle.

The most difficult task here was the erection of the wigwam (see 'Hard Landscaping', pp.166–67). Each of the poles was 5.5m (18ft) long, heavy enough to require three people to lift it, and not exactly easy to handle. Although the poles appeared to be roped together, they were in fact fastened together with a substantial wire hawser threaded through holes drilled in each pole. The structure, when completed, consisted of six poles, and we had to work very closely as a team to assemble and erect it safely. Initially, the first three posts were fixed together at the top of their length while they were still laid on the ground, and a sturdy rope was tied to the top of the poles so that they could be hauled upright (this rope was eventually used to bind the wigwam). The task of hauling up the poles was actually much easier than had been expected. We started by opening up the poles to form an 'A' frame (two poles forming one leg and one forming the other), with two people pulling on the rope and one person on each leg to haul the frame upright and then separate the two poles forming one leg, creating a tripod. To make this operation as safe as possible, the frame was pulled *up* the slope of the garden, which allowed total control of the situation and greatly reduced the chances of anyone getting injured. We had agreed beforehand that if anyone felt they could not lift or hold a pole in place, they must shout a warning and every member of the team would step clear immediately. Thankfully, the need to put our safety contingency into practice did not arise. Each pole was buried 45cm (18in) into the ground to provide added stability, with the base of each one being firmly placed on a section of paving slab to spread the weight, and prevent any sinkage. After the tripod was firmly in position and safe, the three remaining poles were added, their bases dug into position, and their tops wired into place.

Materials and equipment

Sharp sand (5cu m)
Cement (5 bags)
John Innes seed compost
Mulching material (14 x 80 litres)
Old carpet
Growmore fertilizer (10kg)
Resin-coated slow-release fertilizer (2kg)
Dulux Timbercolour 'Black Oak'
Dulux exterior wood stain
Chestnut poles (80 x 2.4m)
Chestnut poles (60 x 2m)
Chestnut posts (6 x 5.5m)
Tannelized wood (25 x 6in x 1in)
Scaffolding planks (5 x 3.5m)
Scaffolding planks (1 x 4.2m)
Railway sleepers (22 x 2.5m)
Woven wicker tunnel
Rope (150m x 16mm)
Rotary mower
Strimmer
Rubbish skip
Sledgehammers
Chainsaw + full safety equipment
Heavy-duty electric hammer-drill

◀ The top part of the Norwich garden provides a functional garden room and a spillover area from the house.

▼ Kirsten's herb garden with Isabelle's den and wigwam in the play area beyond.

▲ A child's sandpit, using railway sleepers as paving.

▼ *Lining the sandpit, the chestnut-pole fence supports climbers and lavender.*

Soft Landscaping

Kirsten's garden presented itself as a generous space in which to create three distinct areas, each with its own function and atmosphere: a produce and utility area for play and sitting out, a meadow with fruit trees, and at the bottom of the garden a play area with the wigwam and the retreat. The planting would be bold but simple, to tie in with the rustic scheme.

The top area of the garden was partially divided off by the chestnut-pole fence, which was planted with strawberry vine and climbing nasturtiums on the lower side and with green ivy lightened by golden hop and honeysuckle to make a screen between Kirsten and her neighbours. The climbers would provide a sense of privacy and also give fruit. The inner garden enclosed by the fence would be planted with an eclectic mix of herbs, flowers and vegetables: taller plants – bergamot, lovage, angelica and fennel – in the back bed, and smaller ones – thyme, oregano and chives – in the angle of the seat. The scent from these aromatic plants would drift into the sitting area. Kirsten interplanted the herbs with sunflowers, Brussels sprouts, coriander and carrots. The sunny wall at the base of the house was linked to the garden with a bold mound of lavender, which would push out from underneath the seat and give summer scent and flowers.

A lavender and rosemary hedge returned from the fence to enclose the potager and frame this area throughout the year. The heat and dry soil were perfect for herbs, which thrive in these conditions. We suggested another vine for the wall of the house to soften the building and once again link it to the garden.

The small area of lawn that was left within the enclosure would be kept for picnics and as a spill-over area from the house – a room outside. A vegetable patch was laid out to frame the fourth side of this area: at the top we planted fruit bushes and rhubarb, and in the lower section Kirsten and Isabelle planned to grow vegetables.

A mown path led from this top enclosed area down into the lower garden as an invitation into the meadow. The juxtaposition of mown path and long grass would give the informal area of the garden the impression that it was intentional and cared for, and make a contrast to the rigid layout of the utility area.

A self-fertile Cox apple and a plum were planted in the meadow on the west side of the garden where shade would be kept to a minimum, and in the grass to the left of the path we planted a clump of tayberry, a loganberry and a thornless blackberry. These were grown on post and rope supports, arranged so that the plants would grow up into a column and cascade down. This was quite unusual, as plants with this type of growth are traditionally trained along wire fences.

Three buddlejas were placed along the fence, with tree lupins to help accentuate the transition from one area to the next. The grassy meadow was cut as low as possible with a rotary mower to enable us to introduce young wildflower plants – meadow cranesbill, greater knapweed and meadow buttercup in random swathes in the driest section, and meadowsweet, cowslip and ragged robin in the shade towards the bottom. This introduction of native plants will be repeated each year, and once they are established the grass will be allowed to grow to about 30–45cm (12–18in), to be cut only twice a year.

To partially screen the wigwam and create a sense of mystery, a clump of hazel was planted in the grass. The wigwam itself was planted with fast-growing orange peel clematis (*Clematis* 'Bill Mackenzie'), which would create a billowing cloud of growth and flower in summer and a mass of silvered seedheads in winter. A large-leaved vine, *Vitis coignetiae*, was added to give a sense of the exotic and for its rampant growth, which would scale the wigwam within two seasons.

Kirsten's retreat was planted very simply with a circle of silver birch. They were placed just 45cm (18in) apart, so that as they grew, competition would keep them relatively small. From the top of the garden the planting would appear as a small wild copse of silver stems; from within, it would be an entirely private space with short grass on the floor and long meadow all around. The close proximity to the overgrown privet hedge linked it to the bottom of the garden. Over the years more shade-loving species such as primroses, honesty and bluebells could be introduced to make it into a delightful mini-glade.

The planting at the bottom of the garden was designed to create a sense of mystery and intrigue for adults and children alike. The cool leafiness and relaxed atmosphere would be a marked contrast to the more formal top end of the garden.

We planted a berry hedge along both sides of the garden. Kirsten did not want a feeling of order or enclosure, so species were chosen which would be allowed to ramble and attain their natural dimensions (approximately 1.5m) – the cut-leaved elder, *Sambucus nigra* f. *laciniata*, which would grow less vigorously than its thuggish cousin, with sweetbriar, dog-roses and the occasional hawthorn. In autumn the hedge would be a riot of berries and fruits for the birds.

The relaxed atmosphere of the garden was retained by a careful choice of plant material, designed to fend mostly for itself. Most of the plants, particularly in the meadow, would be encouraged to take their chances after the first two years of careful tending. The productive part of the garden, though higher-maintenance, would be flexible in the amount of care required.

A large number of plants were introduced into this garden, many of them as 'plugs' – small peat blocks with seedlings growing inside. All the wildflower plants were grown in this way, and because they were so small they were planted last of all so that we reduced the risk of treading on them. Cutting down and clearing away the grass and brambles was essential for the long-term establishment of the wildflowers; they usually thrive in impoverished soil, but not where there is too much competition.

Many of the fruit trees and bushes were 'bare root' (grown in the open ground), and had been dug up and sent to us by mail-order. These plants were still in their winter dormancy when they arrived and were ideal for transplanting. They were all given a thorough watering immediately after planting, to help them establish as quickly as possible.

Because of the low rainfall in this part of the country, we were well aware of the need for water conservation. However, water was vital to the young plants until they had established firm roots into the soil, and with this in mind, as many as possible were mulched with a layer of organic matter. This helps not only to reduce the need for watering, but also to prevent weed seedlings emerging. In the seating area at the top of the garden, as an experiment, we planted a row of lavender bushes through an old carpet, which we disguised with an organic mulch.

Plants and seeds

Betula pendula
Buddleja 'Black Knight'
Buddleja 'Dartmouth'
Buddleja 'White Profusion'
Clematis 'Bill Mackenzie'
Corylus 'Red Skin Filbert'
Eccremocarpus scaber
Geranium pratense
Hedera helix
Humulus lupulus 'Aureus'
Ilex aquifolium
Lathyrus odoratus
Lavandula angustifolia
Lupinus arboreus
Lonicera periclymenum
    'Graham Thomas'
Monarda 'Cambridge Scarlet'
Rosa rubiginosa
Rosmarinus 'Miss Jessop's
    Upright'
Sambucus nigra f. laciniata
Viburnum opulus
Vitis coignetiae
Vitis vinifera 'Fragola'

Apple tree 'Queen Cox'
Blackberry 'Merton Thornless'
Plum tree 'Victoria'
Loganberry 'Thornless'

Rhubarb
Tayberry

Angelica
Bergamot
Chives
Coriander
Fennel
Lemon balm
Lovage
Marjoram
Oregano
Parsley
Sage
Sorrel
Thyme

Artichoke (globe)
Artichoke (Jerusalem)
Beetroot
Broad beans
Carrot
Courgette
Gourds
Potato (early)
Ruby chard
Runner beans
Tomato

▶ *Kirsten's herb garden.*

Wendy and Leslie

A Coastal Garden
Sussex

The Client

The occupants of this property, Wendy and Leslie, are designers who work long hours and spend frequent periods of time away from home on various assignments, not only in the United Kingdom but also in various other parts of the world. These periods are interspersed with blocks of time of irregular duration spent working from home.

Spending long periods of time living in hotels or rented accommodation makes them not only appreciate, but actually treasure, the time spent in their own home and garden, particularly after travelling long distances to get there. This kind of lifestyle creates pressures that make the seclusion of the garden important for relaxing and unwinding, an ideal environment in which to recharge their batteries before jetting off to the next assignment. The amount of time they can spend on garden maintenance is very varied, and any plants must be able to fend for themselves while their owners are away.

Wendy and Leslie were faced with problems relating to their garden. There were the obvious environmental problems of fearsome winds and gravelly free-draining soil, coupled with the impact of the surrounding landscape. They felt they needed a new vision to help them make an inroad into the garden. As Leslie put it, he could design anything within the confines of a square, like his textile designs, but felt daunted by the

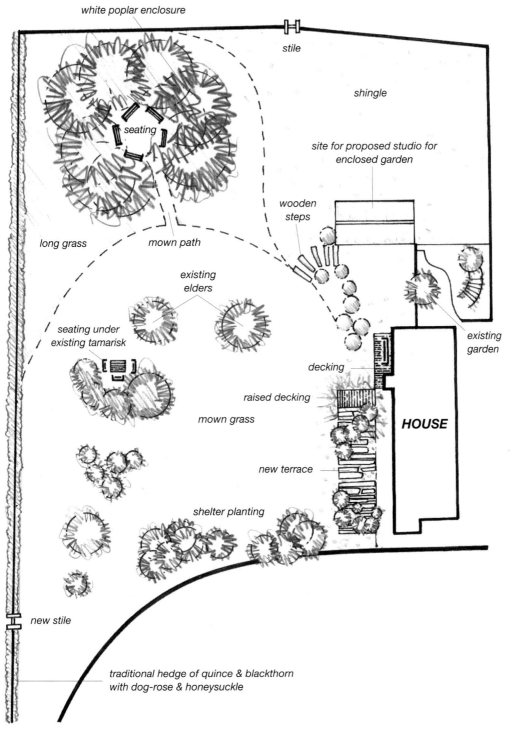

white poplar enclosure

stile

shingle

seating

site for proposed studio for
enclosed garden

wooden
steps

long grass

mown path

existing
elders

seating under
existing tamarisk

decking

existing
garden

raised decking

mown grass

HOUSE

new terrace

shelter planting

new stile

traditional hedge of quince & blackthorn
with dog-rose & honeysuckle

garden that lay beyond the small enclosure they had already tackled.

They knew the limitations of the site, with its exposure problems and its resident colony of rabbits, and were quite happy to continue the theme they had already established, with driftwood set into the shingle, rather than to introduce new materials. They felt that the landscape spoke for itself and did not want to create anything too contrived, yet almost paradoxically they were fascinated by sculptural plants, which reminded them of plants they had seen in America – they felt that the alien atmosphere of their garden could be the perfect place for plants which one would not usually see in cultivation.

Leslie in particular had an interest in plants and was keen to increase the range. He felt that at some point in the future he would like to make a formal area, though they were aware that this was at odds with the informality of the landscape. They had a strong aesthetic sense but had become discouraged by the situation, partly through an awareness of the garden's inherent problems and partly through a familiarity with the landscape, which they found almost enough in itself. They wanted a new look but they were keen to keep a tight rein on developments so that the results would tie in with what they had envisaged.

The Diagnosis

Because this garden was so near to the coast there were considerable constraints, and many of the plants chosen were selected on the basis of being tough and very hardy. Paramount in this instance, unusually, was tolerance to exposure from biting, often salt-laden winds, rather than to low temperatures. The very mention of the word soil had Wendy and Leslie falling about in fits of laughter,

since for many years they had struggled valiantly to introduce new plants and grow them on what could accurately be described as the waste material from a gravel-pit. The rabbits greedily welcomed the newly introduced plants and immediately set about devouring them before they had a chance to become established, and, to make matters even worse, the land sloped steeply away from the house, which made working on the site difficult, especially on the loose, ever-moving shingle.

Both Wendy and Leslie appreciate plants and like to grow them but would never have described themselves as keen or accomplished gardeners. They both felt that in some respects they had an impossible dream, wanting a garden with a range of plants that were both interesting and capable of growing in their bleak and exposed location. The key to this project lay in being able to overcome the topographical and soil-structural difficulties and create a terrace. We knew we could not use a 'cut

*▲ **The hard lines of the timber used on the decking are soon softened by the new planting.***

*◀ (Top) **The coast of east Sussex: beautiful but exposed and often windswept.***

*◀ (Bottom) **Dan, Leslie, Wendy and Brad relaxing in the coastal garden.***

and fill' technique to create the terrace, because if we took away the grass which was binding the surface of the bank, we would have had tonnes of loose shingle to deal with, and no chance of building a terrace on what was left. Of all the gardens in the series, this garden was in many respects the most taxing to build physically, due to the sheer bulk and size of the materials we used; we were, however, able to follow the design brief quite closely. The recycled timber was perfect, just what we wanted, and, even better, it was free; our only cost was for haulage to Wendy and Leslie's garden from the work area the National Rivers Authority staff were using along the coast.

One unusual problem occurred on the day we visited the site to select the timber. This visit happened to coincide with one of the worst storms in this area for many years, and we had to make a very hasty tactical withdrawal as conditions worsened.

At the end of the terrace, a raised deck was to be built as a seating area under the shade of a large tamarisk tree. The tree had two trunks which would emerge through the surface of the deck once it was completed, so we had to ensure that the deck could take the weight of a person standing close to the base of the tree, but at the same time make sure we did not damage the roots or trunks of the tree itself. The main structural supports were actually built around the tree in such a way as to leave room for the trunks to continue expanding for a good many years to come. This tree was a dominant feature within the existing garden and we were keen to retain it in the new landscape if at all possible, as it would provide the look of maturity which is so important until new introductions have become established.

A square concreted area immediately outside the side door of the house was covered with a wooden 'duckboard' placed directly on to the concrete. This was not in the original brief, but the old cracked concrete looked so out of context with what we had built in such close proximity to it that we added this extra feature rather than allow the overall effect of the project to be spoilt.

Hard Landscaping

The terrace that we planned would make the steeply sloping site more accessible to walk through and much easier to garden, and because the site was so exposed and bare there was no real clearance work to do before the construction work could begin.

In order to support the earth dam, a retaining wall had to be built; this would allow the formation of the terrace and enable us to create a garden on split levels. This retaining wall would be holding back several tonnes of soil and shingle, and to support this considerable weight the upright supports had to go several feet into the ground.

The material used for the terrace needed to be in keeping with its maritime environment, and we chose large sections of reclaimed sea-washed timber which had previously been used to form part of the coastal sea defences just down the coast. These beautiful, weather-worn, cracked and gnarled timbers were the ideal material for a coastal garden, and their size was perfectly in proportion with the scale of the garden.

Because of the size of the posts (40cm/16in square) and the fact that we were working on a shingle bank, knocking them into the ground was not a feasible option. Trying to dig out, by hand, shingle which just continues to collapse back into the hole is pretty futile and a very demoralizing occupation. We knew we had to try a mechanical solution, but did not want to take out larger holes than necessary if we could possibly avoid it. We took a 'calculated gamble', opting for a hydraulically powered auger, mounted on a JCB excavator. The first hole we took out was a complete disaster – as the auger was withdrawn from the ground, all the earth and shingle just spun off the bit. The JCB driver then told us that he had not used an auger before, so over a large mug of coffee we discussed the problem with him, and his help proved invaluable; he kept trying different methods and then stopping so that we could examine the effectiveness of each. He soon discovered that the most effective method was to insert the auger to its full depth into the shingle while it turned at its slowest possible speed. When the maximum depth was reached, he would stop the auger rotating and lift it out of the ground, pulling a 'plug' of shingle with it.

Once the holes had been made, the upright posts had to be quickly inserted into the holes as carefully as possible before the surrounding shingle dried out and started to slip back in. As the smallest post we inserted required four people to lift it, this was no easy task, bearing in mind that we had to lift and move the posts on a soil shingle mix which was collapsing beneath our feet.

The retaining wall was also made from reclaimed sea-washed timber, and here we had a different problem: these planks were very sound structurally, although quite old, but were all of different lengths, and we had to devise a way of adding strength and stability to the sections without spoiling the overall effect. The solution was found in the form of sheets of marine plywood, which were fastened behind the reclaimed timber to retain the soil and help to even out the pressure along the entire terrace; the horizontal planks of the terrace could also be fastened against the plywood, so lending extra support.

The upright posts had to go at least 1m (3ft) into the ground, and due to their size and thickness we had to use a chainsaw to do most of the cutting to length.

Before any plants were used, imported topsoil was added to the terrace area. When we were excavating the holes to position the main posts for the terrace wall, we were surprised to discover that the shingle was only 60cm (2ft) deep and was actually overlying clay. This clay was quite wet, despite both the very dry weather conditions and the fact that we were almost at the top of the steepest slope in the garden. This discovery was particularly encouraging, as we now knew that once the plants had become

---

Materials and equipment

Marine ply (2.4m x 1.2m)
Timber (tannalized 4in x 2in)
Timber (untreated 6in x 1in)
Garden loam (5cu m)
Mulching material (14 x 80 litres)
Recycled timber (ex groins from sea defences)
JCB excavator with auger fitting
Chainsaw + full safety equipment
Cordless drills
Slow-release fertilizer

---

established and put down some roots they would have a very good chance of survival.

Soft Landscaping

Wendy and Leslie faced not only the harshness of blasting sea winds and poor free-draining gravel as soil, but also the ongoing problem of the rabbits, though over the years they had learnt that some plants, such as helichrysum and phormium, seemed immune to these problems. The area chosen to be the first part of the development had two advantages: a degree of protection from the house and a natural bank, which we re-landscaped so that it would be easier to keep the rabbits out.

More advantages presented themselves immediately. The tamarisk was an obvious focal point, with its gnarled growth and potential for giving a degree of shade in summer. The views out over the magnificent landscape prompted us to limit the 'gardened' area to immediately around the house, anchoring anything man-made to the building.

The design would be viewed through the living-room windows, and the planting was kept relatively low and gauzy so that the landscape beyond could

still be seen through it. As the land bleached blond in summer, the new terrace would be planted with a selection of plants which would reach their climax in high summer and continue through into the autumn, the winter shapes of many of the plants remaining until bashed down by the winds.

The key plant on the new terrace was obviously the tamarisk. The wooden deck had been constructed around its twin trunks, and little was planted underneath in the shade. Wendy and Leslie brought pots of dark liquorice-coloured aeonium around from the glasshouse and kept them here for summer interest. At the other end of the terrace we retained the windblown pines for shelter and to give a dark background, and continued the green-grey *Eleagnus* x *ebbingii* down from the terrace into the garden for further wind protection. This established area was used as the anchor for the new planting.

An old iron cauldron was placed as a focal point and filled with water to reflect the sky. Some wild

▲ *(Left)* **Eryngium, or 'sea-holly', was a natural choice for this garden.**

▲ *(Right)* **The deck provides an observation platform and shade from the tamarisk tree.**

◀ **Despite the naturally harsh conditions posed by a coastal site, it is still possible to create a vibrant blend of colour and shape using the right plant material.**

reeds were brought up from the ditch at the bottom of the garden, to bring the landscape up close to the house and for their wonderful movement in the constant breeze. Wendy and Leslie were keen to use some strong architectural foliage for impact. We bought in the largest *Agave americana* we could find to be the key plant. When planted large, agaves are perfectly hardy by the coast in a relatively frost-free situation as long as the soil is free-draining. These were perfect conditions.

The next key plants in the scheme were the brooms, which, with their reduced leaf surface, were ideal for these conditions. Three *Genista aetnensis* were planted close to the pines – their growth, wiry and almost transparent, would partially mask the drive. They were echoed further into the garden with a clump of Spanish broom, *Spartium junceum*, for its similar growth and scented gold flowers. We interplanted these with inky-purple *Buddleja* 'Black Knight' and a random planting of the Californian tree poppy, *Romneya coulteri*, which is ideal in dry, free-draining conditions. The romneya would run through the terrace eventually, pushing up to 2m (6ft) with silvery leaves and flat white flowers like crumpled tissue paper.

The next layer of planting was the evergreen contingent. Between the wooden planks we planted drifts of purple sage in bold groups. The colour was excellent with the shingle. *Stipa tenuissima*, a low clump-forming grass, was scattered over the whole area to give a continuity, concentrated in some parts and isolated in others. In winter its growth would become a bleached pale brown, and in summer its delicate tasselled flowers would provide a constant motion in the breeze and give the whole terrace the impression of water ruffled by the wind.

The next groups of plants to be introduced made an important focus of interest. A large drift of electric-blue *Perovskia* 'Blue Spire' to soften the blue-green architectural foliage of the agave was placed first, with clumps of navy-blue *Agapanthus campanulatus* 'Isis' to continue the colour through. A clump of three honey spurge were planted almost in isolation, to link up to the tamarisk. Their acid-green evergreen foliage and mound-like habit would connect the tamarisk to the rest of the scheme.

Smaller, though equally important, details were added as random elements to give the scheme a self-sown feel: bronze fennel, three giant *Eryngium agavifolium*, and thirty plants of *Eryngium giganteum*, a monocarpic sea-holly which would seed itself from year to year, its flowers brilliant silver, bleaching to parchment-white in winter. We added maiden pinks to give magenta splashes of colour, with *Thymus* 'Silver Posie' in crevices between the planks, and finally we sowed mixed eschscholzia in the gaps for instant colour and brilliant orange blooms through the summer. Below the terrace the bank was stabilized with the silver dune grass, *Leymus arenarius*, and teasels and opium poppies were encouraged to seed freely in order to blend the terrace into the wildness of the garden beyond.

The brilliant light conditions would bring out the colour of many of the silver plants, and the sea breezes provided another element, captured by the motion of the grasses. The scheme would be both delicate and subtle, and from a distance would not register as an ornamental garden. Within the garden, however, there would be a constantly changing matrix of plants which would be a focus and at the same time would not be a distraction from the vivid landscape all around.

The large quantity of imported soil used to fill the terrace area and raise the level had shingle incorporated into it. This was done so that all the soil in the terrace was similar to the native soil, and had similar physical properties and characteristics. It is particularly important to form a link between imported soil and that which already exists, otherwise the two will dry out at different rates, with the topsoil (where the plants are) drying out more quickly, harming the establishing plants.

Most of the plants we used in this garden were grown in containers, and we did not tease out the roots when planting (as is sometimes recommended), as we wanted to minimize root disturbance.

During planting, generous quantities of fertilizer were incorporated to compensate for the low nutritional value of the thin impoverished soil. A generous handful of slow-release fertilizer was scattered around each plant as it was firmed into position, and each rootball was given a good watering immediately after planting. Not only did this settle the soil around the plants but the moisture also activated the fertilizer and started to feed the plant immediately. Any plants we found with dry rootballs were submerged in a bucket of water until the compost around the roots was thoroughly wet.

After planting, a thick 5cm (2in) mulch of organic matter was applied over the soil to reduce water loss and prevent weed seeds germinating. To speed up this operation, the smaller plants were covered with large plant-pots before the mulch was added; this prevented them being smothered, and when the pots were removed the plants were left exposed and free from mulch and dirt on their leaves. All the plants were mulched with shingle soon after planting to blend in with the surroundings, to help prevent moisture loss, and to reduce germination of weed seeds.

Plants and seeds

Agapanthus campanulatus 'Isis'
Agave americanum
Allium christophii
Asparagus officinalis
Buddleja 'Black Knight'
Buddleja 'Lochinch'
Cortaderia selloana 'Sunningdale Silver'
Dasylirion gracile
Dianthus deltoides
Erigeron karvinskianus
Eryngium agavifolium
Eryngium giganteum
Eschscholzia californica
Euphorbia mellifera
Foeniculum vulgare 'Purpureum'
Genista aetnensis
Leymus arenarius
Linum narbonense
Origanum 'Herrenhausen'
Perovskia 'Blue Spire'
Romneya coulteri
Rosmarinus officinalis
Salvia officinalis 'Purpurescens'
Santolina 'Edward Bowles'
Spartium junceum
Stipa tenuissima
Thymus 'Silver Posie'
Yucca glauca

◀ *Aeoniums lifted from the glasshouse for the summer*
to add interest.
▼ *The wooden decking of the new terrace was*
constructed around the existing tamarisk tree.

Sarah and Oliver

A Wild Garden
Buckinghamshire

The Client

The occupants of this house, Sarah and Oliver, divide their working lives equally between their respective businesses in London and working from home, with the eventual goal of working from home almost full-time. Their home was originally the farmhouse to a working farm, and it still retains views over open countryside, in a very rural setting. Both are interested in gardening, but have very different views on how they would like the garden to look. A compromise was called for. Low maintenance is an absolute must here, and by opting for a semi-natural effect, where the grass needs cutting only a few times each year, a well-managed, natural effect is achieved with very little input.

Sarah and Oliver wanted a retreat from busy city life, and by the time we visited them they had finished renovating the seventeenth-century farmhouse and were eager to start work on the garden. They liked the idea of developing the garden over a period, but were anxious that it should not rule their lives in terms of maintenance. Sarah had a strong leaning towards an informal style, while Oliver was more concerned that the garden should be a place in which he could relax and entertain. They were both keen, however, that the garden should blend with the surrounding countryside and that it should not feel remotely suburban.

During renovations the area around the house had suffered, and in

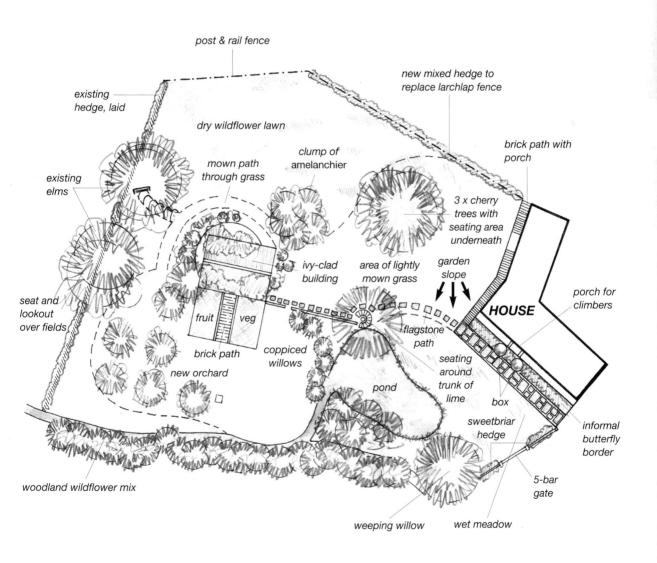

post & rail fence

new mixed hedge to replace larchlap fence

existing hedge, laid

dry wildflower lawn

brick path with porch

existing elms

mown path through grass

clump of amelanchier

3 x cherry trees with seating area underneath

ivy-clad building

area of lightly mown grass

garden slope

porch for climbers

seat and lookout over fields

fruit   veg

flagstone path

HOUSE

brick path

coppiced willows

seating around trunk of lime

box

new orchard

pond

sweetbriar hedge

informal butterfly border

woodland wildflower mix

5-bar gate

weeping willow

wet meadow

the winter most of it had become a mud-bath. Sarah had saved a small area in front of the house from the builders, who wanted to make a gravel drive, and she saw this as having potential as a wet meadow, leading down to the small spring under a weeping willow, where she could grow fritillaries and wetland species. Beyond that she saw the garden as an area for wildflowers, with paths cut through long grass and plants to attract butterflies and birds – a place to delight the five senses.

Oliver wanted a distinct area of lawn that would lead right up to the house, and wanted to use the cherry saplings at the highest point of the garden as a possible site for a patio. A small derelict barn was being developed as a roost for an owl, and behind this area they thought there could be room for a small orchard and a vegetable garden. They both felt that

the spring-fed pond should be enlarged so that there was a good view of water from the house. They liked the willow beside the existing pond, and the feel of slightly unkempt abandon which the garden already possessed when they first saw it. They realized that this might well have to be sacrificed in order to create a managed 'wild' garden, and were quite happy to hire large equipment to level out what had been left by the builders. They saw the garden as a long-term investment.

The Diagnosis

In the main, this garden would be kept as wild as possible. Nature would be the dominant element, with large areas of wildflowers, and the garden would merge with the surrounding farmland.

The slope leading up from the house would be graded, then sown with grass and wildflower seeds to provide a country meadow atmosphere. To allow views out over the countryside, the hedge along the western boundary would be laid in a traditional fashion, and a berry-rich hedge of native species would be planted.

Close to the house, a more formal theme would be

achieved by having small areas of ornamental planting with a wide flagstone path providing access to the front of the house from the road. This would leave space for a border between the pathway and the wall of the house, allowing the opportunity for planting shrubs, perennials and climbers selected to encourage bees and butterflies.

To the south of this path a wet meadow would lead down to the sloping edges of the pond, where marginal aquatics would be planted. In order to accommodate the extension to the pond, the old weeping willow would be removed and replaced with

a younger tree in a slightly different place. When the water of the pond reached the optimum level, the water-loving marginals could be planted in their correct positions.

We had two problems on this site. Both concerned water flow and water levels, and led to a slight change of plan. The first occurred within a week of the excavation work being done, when Oliver (now back at work in London) received a telephone call from their next-door neighbours, who thought they could hear running water inside the house. It transpired that a piped spring ran under the house and into the pond, and we soon realized that due to the very wet soil conditions, the JCB excavator had sunk into the soil much lower than it would normally do; the pipe carrying the spring had been crushed and the flow to the pond was blocked. This blockage came very close to causing a serious flood in the house, and all from a spring which no one knew even existed. We overcame this problem by digging a trench and re-routeing the spring into the pond through a new pipe.

The second problem was, incredibly, lack of water, or at least lack of a high enough water level. This was essential for the high water-table needed to create a wet meadow area. We also had to raise the water within the pond to its intended level in order to create the ideal conditions for the marginal plants to thrive. The solution we settled on was to build a sluice gate by the outflow, consisting of timber positioned horizontally, to restrict the flow and ensure that the water level could rise.

Hard Landscaping

The dominant feature in this garden was not a structure as such, but the expansion of a spring-fed stream into a large pond in a very natural setting.

Because of the size and scale of this project, we had to resort to the use of earth-moving machinery to work on the rough levels before we could get a true indication of what we had to work with.

The earthworks were started on a wet and miserable day in February, when a member of the JCB Excavators 'Dancing Diggers' display team brought down a very clean demonstration machine to dig out the ditch and create the pond. Considering the ground conditions and our difficulty in slithering over 60cm (2ft) deep, water-filled ruts, the man with the 'Dancing Digger' did us proud, but his machine certainly did not stay clean for more than about five minutes. He managed to create the contours for the pond, making several unexpected discoveries in the process: he uncovered old bedsteads, rotting corrugated-iron sheets, cattle-feeders and glass, and we soon realized that the intended site for our lovely country pond had, in fact, been the farm dump.

As work progressed and we went down deeper, we found a 30cm (1ft) thick layer of brown peat-like material – the bottom level of the original pond. This peaty layer consisted of generations of old rotted leaves which had settled along the floor of the pond. We eventually discovered from old maps that this was actually the site of a pond which had been used as a water-hole for cattle, but had been abandoned, only to be filled in many years later.

We had to remove an old weeping willow tree in order to increase the pond area, but we took hardwood cuttings from it, to create 'son of willow tree' on the opposite side of the pond.

The slope leading up from the house into the garden was very uneven, full of perennial weeds, and contained a large heap of rich blue clay, the waste from the hole dug when a new septic tank had been installed the previous year. This area was graded to create an even slope, similar to a rolling country meadow; the clay was mixed with the subsoil beneath, and the topsoil was put back over the graded site. As part of this grading process, a large half-dead conifer was removed and laid at the edge of the site, eventually providing fuel for one of the open fires in the house.

Soft Landscaping

Sarah and Oliver were keen that the garden should be very much part of the countryside – it should retain a wild and slightly unkempt atmosphere and be home to wildflowers and local fauna. The design was carefully worked out so that the garden became progressively more wild as it moved away from the house – all the ornamental material was kept close to the building, and forms of wild species, such as the bronze-leaved elder and the amber-berried *Viburnum opulus* 'Xanthocarpum', were used further into the garden as constant reference to the countryside beyond.

A simple flagstone path providing access to the front door divided a wet meadow leading down to the pond from a border of butterfly subjects near the house. The two were united by a random border of camassia and scarlet oriental poppies to give a brilliant welcome in May and June. The wildflower garden would not be as purist in this section of the garden – it was important that the ornamental should flow into the wild.

The butterfly border was planted simply, with a bold mix of *Sedum* 'Autumn Joy' for its autumn flower and winter skeletons and *Aster frikartii* 'Mönch'. *Buddleja* 'Lochinch' provided height and silvery winter buds, and *Lavandula spica* winter bulk. A white wisteria and a vine were planted in the second season to clothe the house wall. Two box

trees were added as a full stop on either side of the door. They would be allowed to grow at least 1m (3ft) in diameter and would ideally be encouraged as rough clipped spheres.

A sweetbriar and honeysuckle hedge ran along the boundary fence separating the car-parking space from the wet meadow, which was sown with a special wetland mix containing ragged robin, cowslips, and fritillaries. More fritillaries were added as bulbs, in naturalistic drifts leading down to the pond. The pond edge was sown with a wetland wildflower mix and interplanted with tall purple loosestrife, meadowsweet and a mixture of flowering natives to give constant interest. In the second season we introduced water aquatics and the native white water-lily.

The wet meadow, which would be left as long grass until June, was divided off by a large sweep of rough-cut grass which moved in an arc to the brow of the hill, providing a gentle sweep into the garden. The camassias were brought further into the garden and planted under groupings of viburnum and *Rosa moyesii*, which would eventually form large clumps in

---

Materials and equipment

Mulching material (14 x 80 litres)
Resin-coated slow-release fertilizer (2kg)
JCB excavator
Rotovator (2)
Rubbish skip
Topsoil (5cu m)
Knapsack sprayer + safety clothing
Glyphosate weedkiller
Metal tubes (32mm x 45cm)
Metal tie-straps (5)
Mild steel rods (2 x 5m)
Casauron G (dichlobenil) granular weedkiller

▲ *(Top)* **A wattle seat, well sited in an area of dappled shade.**

▲ **Papaver orientale *'Marcus Perry'*, an important feature of the soft landscaping.**

▶ **Fritillaria meleagris *in the wet meadow.***

the long grass and link the old outhouse with the garden in the foreground. In the first season, we removed the larchlap fence dividing off the neighbours and replaced it with a mixed native hedge which connected more satisfactorily with the landscape beyond. This had the immediate effect of allowing the eye to travel out over the fields.

In the first season the dry meadow at the end of the garden was sown with a dryland mix of wildflowers and interplanted with perennial plugs such as bistort, wild marjoram and cranesbill in sweeping drifts. This meadow, in marked contrast to the rough-cut lawn, would be left long for the majority of the summer, and a sweeping path would be cut into it to lead to the new orchard area and the retreat.

A large clump of *Amelanchier canadensis* were planted at the junction of the cut and the uncut grass to hold the eye and create a sense of mystery and distance beyond. More native shrubs were planted around the outbuilding to link it to the garden, and a small orchard and wood-edged vegetable patch was made at the rear of the barn. The ground underneath the elm trees was cleared and sown with a woodland mix containing foxgloves, campion and chelidonium.

The key with this garden was always to think big, planting in bold drifts as if all the plants had been thrown down by nature and arrived in that position on their own. All the plants were chosen for their wild appearance, even the white rambling roses which would be allowed to climb among the ivy over the outbuilding, and with the exception of the buddlejas and the plants in the immediate vicinity of the house there would be nothing that would need pruning or look as if it had been overly manicured. For a sense of the wild to predominate, a relaxed attitude would be nine-tenths of the story.

The second visit to this garden, almost two

raise the pond to its intended level, consisted of several sections of timber positioned horizontally to ensure that the water level could rise. The advantage of using several narrower sections of wood rather than one large piece is that if you need to open the sluice, with the water pressure behind it, it is much easier to move small sections of timber, rather than one large one.

The whole garden area was thoroughly cultivated to create a fine tilth for seed sowing. This was perhaps the biggest individual task, as the ground was very rutted and uneven as a result of the excavation work we had carried out earlier. To make matters worse, the soil had dried out to the extent of baking quite hard, which made using the rotary cultivator we had hired a rather energetic and interesting pastime. These cultivations revealed copious quantities of stones, broken bricks, fragments of glass and slate, all of which had to be collected, removed in a wheelbarrow and dumped. Over a two-day period we removed sufficient material to fill a large skip.

The soil in the wet meadow area was so poor that we imported a lorry-load of topsoil to improve the conditions. After completing all the rotary cultivation, the entire garden was skilfully raked and graded by students from the Berkshire College of Agriculture – the process took seven of them a whole day, but the end result was well worth the time and effort.

The following day, the grass seed was sown. Half the seed was scattered across the area in one direction, and the remaining half was sown at right angles to the first. This is a very simple way of ensuring that the seed is evenly distributed over the whole site. We knew we had to try to protect the seed until it had germinated, so we used seed containing a bird-repellent – rather than act as a

months later, showed the pond three-quarters full, with a dense covering of green blanket-weed. In order to combat the blanket-weed, which was completely suffocating all life in the pond, we threw in a bag of barley straw. This prevents the blanket-weed getting the nitrogen which is in the pond, so that gradually it stops growing and disappears.

The sluice gate that was built by the outflow, to

Plants and seeds

Amelanchier canadensis
Apples (6 of each): 'Ellison's Orange'
    and 'Spartan'
Aster x *frikartii* 'Mönch'
Buddleja 'Lochinch'
Caltha palustris
Clematis viticella 'Alba Luxurians'
Cornus sanguinea
Crataegus monogyna
Filipendula ulmaria
Fritillaria meleagris
Iris pseudacorus
Ilex aquifolium
Lathyrus latifolius
Lavandula angustifolia
Lavandula spica
Lonicera periclymenum
Myosotis palustris
Papaver orientale 'Marcus Perry'
Rosa moyesii
Rosa rubiginosa
Salix alba
Salix alba var. *vitellina*
Sedum 'Autumn Joy'
Viburnum opulus 'Xanthocarpum'
Vitis vinifera 'Fragola'
Vitis vinifera 'Purpurea'
Grass seed (25kg)

---

poison, this makes the seed unappetizing to the birds and they spit it out. We also recycled some old polythene bags, making them into 'bird-scarers' to discourage interest in the newly seeded areas.

Much of the planting proved to be quite difficult in the hard and dry soil conditions. The hedging plants, and most of the plants which were not growing in containers, were stored in wet polythene bags until the very moment of planting. We dipped some of the drier containerized plants in the pond to keep them moist, standing them half-submerged along the water's edge until they were planted. The herbaceous perennials were watered-in immediately after planting, and a thick layer of mulch was applied after the water had soaked in.

When we planted the marginal plants around the edges of the pond, we had a completely different problem. The soil was very wet, and we kept sinking into the soft bank to such an extent that at one stage we resorted to working in pairs so that we could pull one another out of the mud when it was time to move on to the next section.

Year 2

When we first started work on this garden, we knew that because of its size, we could not possibly complete this project in one year. The best we could really hope for was to provide a framework for Sarah and Oliver to work with.

They had continued the work we had started, sowing the wildflower mixtures we had left for them and tackling a hard-landscaping project of their own at the far end of the garden. Between them, they had constructed a hard-standing area made from bricks laid on a sand sub-base, to form the platform for a garden seat. On summer evenings they would sit and look back across the garden towards the house, or down over the fields into the surrounding countryside. What they really wanted from us at this stage was practical help and suggestions on how to progress with their garden, and ideas on what to do next.

As part of the second stage of this project, we built an apple arch. Sarah had been inspired by one she had seen at Gunnersbury Park on the outskirts of London, and she had produced photographs to show us what she had in mind. We marked out the line that the arch was intended to follow; it was to be arranged in a slight curve so that only about a quarter of the far opening was visible when viewed from either end. The idea is that the viewer's natural curiosity draws them into the arch to get a better view of what is beyond.

The arch was constructed from 13mm (½ in) mild-steel rods, bent over to give a span of 2.4m (8ft) wide and about 2.5m (8½ft) high at the ridge. The length of the arch consisted of eight hoops, each one spaced 1m (3ft) apart, and to give the structure strength and rigidity, five metal tie-straps were bolted to the metal hoops, with the top one forming the ridge of the structure.

In order to make adjustment and levelling easier, we placed 45cm (18in) long metal tubes into the ground and the base of each hoop was slotted into the tube. The hoops were fixed into position by the tension created when the hoops were bent over to form the arch.

The apple trees were planted alongside the arch: 'Ellisons Orange', a mid-season apple which is crisp and juicy with a distinct aniseed flavour to it, but has a tendency to slip into biennial bearing (cropping alternate years), and 'Spartan', which is an apple of Canadian origin with a reputation as a regular cropper, but with fruit which tend to be on the small side. Both these cultivars are classed as moderately vigorous with an upright habit, making them ideal for training over an arch, and as their flowering periods overlap quite considerably, they will be ideal for pollinating one another.

To cover the arch while the apples were growing, we planted the small white-flowered *Clematis viticella* 'Alba Luxurians'.

On this return visit, it was interesting to observe just how much things had changed with the planting. Most of them had started to mature, but the amount of progress was quite mixed. The pond had improved tremendously, with many of the marginal plants now spreading into the water, and the grass now stabilizing the sloping banks down to the water's edge. The rose hedge growing by the front fence had doubled in size over a ten-month period, and the buddleja growing alongside the path was doing so well it had started to overwhelm other plants nearby. The native hedge which ran along the neighbour's boundary had not fared so well; being at the highest and sunniest point in the garden, these plants had obviously struggled through the long, hot summer.

Sarah had become so interested in gardening that she had started to attend courses being offered by Capel Manor College of Enfield at one of their out-centres in south-west London. This had developed her desire to grow her own vegetables on a 'deep-bed system', and she had already started preparing the ground by obtaining plenty of farmyard manure, in order to grow her food as organically as possible.

We undertook a series of maintenance operations and carried out a small amount of new planting. We gave the rose hedge quite a severe pruning, cutting it down to 30cm (1ft) so that it would shoot from the bottom to form a thick bushy hedge. We followed up by giving the hedge a good feed with a slow-release fertilizer, which would keep it well nourished for most of the coming year. We dug up about half the buddleja by the path to leave space for everything else to establish and grow. The native hedge did not need pruning, but we gave it a feed with a slow-release fertilizer and applied a soil-acting weedkiller. This was applied as a granular formulation of Casuron G (dichlobenil), and because the hedge was not really established, we used this chemical at only 25 per cent of the recommended rate. This was done to prevent the chemical harming the hedge while still

giving us reasonable weed control.

Now that the pond had settled down and the natural balance of the pond-life was establishing, we were ready for the next stage of development. This involved planting some additional marginal plants and aquatics. Oliver had set his heart on having a water-lily, and this was duly planted by placing the plant clump in an open-meshed sack and gently throwing it into the right spot in the pond, where it would settle into position.

▲ *Sarah and Oliver relax with their dogs by the pond.*
▶ *One year on and already the garden has taken on an established look with ox-eye daisies, buddlejas and poppies.*

Judy and Ciarán

A Gulf-Stream Garden
Cornwall

The Client

Judy, Ciarán and Flint (a massive Irish wolfhound) share a beautiful
terraced house overlooking a bay near Penzance in Cornwall. The house
is cut into the hillside, so that the front and rear gardens are on different
levels from the house; the rear garden is several metres higher than the
ground floor of the house, and the front garden several metres lower.

Judy is a very good musician who used to sing professionally with a
group, and the front room on the ground floor is filled with musical
instruments. She is the keen gardener in the partnership – for a time she
worked on a local nursery growing and selling plants, a job she
thoroughly enjoyed. Ciarán is a carpenter; he has spent a number of
years working in the construction industry and, at the present time,
builds pole-houses for clients in the south-west.

They had made modest inroads into the garden, with gifts and
purchases from the nursery which had already set a subtropical theme.
They wanted an area that would look out to the bay beyond and, in
contrast, a jungly, engulfing dell of foliage, with heavy growth and scent
for warm summer evenings. They wanted the garden to feel like the
nearby fern-dell, an almost prehistoric experience – Ciarán wanted it to
be 'Jurassic' in atmosphere. They were interested in the extraordinary
forms of foliage that could potentially be grown in the area rather than in
flowers and colour, and wanted a garden of contrast and excitement.

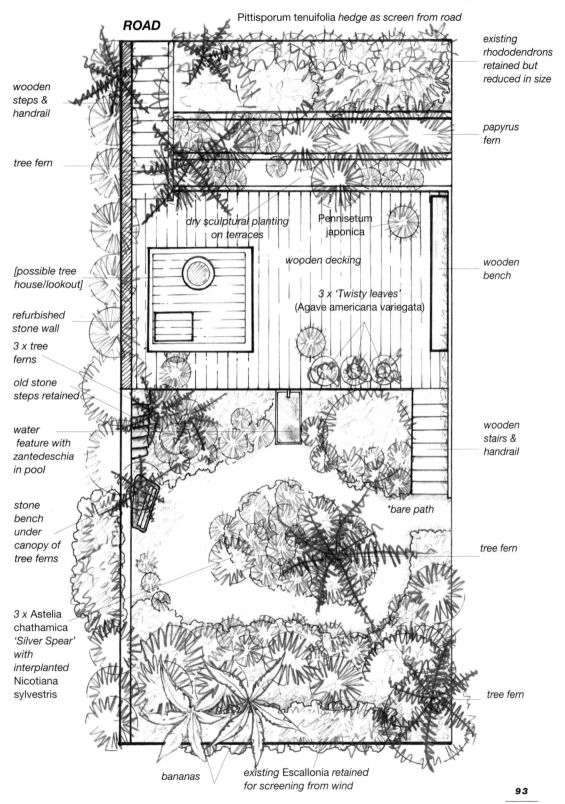

ROAD

Pittisporum tenuifolia *hedge as screen from road*

existing
rhododendrons
retained but
reduced in size

wooden
steps &
handrail

papyrus
fern

tree fern

dry sculptural planting
on terraces

Pennisetum
japonica

wooden decking

wooden
bench

[possible tree
house/lookout]

3 x 'Twisty leaves'
(Agave americana variegata)

refurbished
stone wall

3 x tree
ferns

old stone
steps retained

water
feature with
zantedeschia
in pool

wooden
stairs &
handrail

*bare path

stone
bench
under
canopy of
tree ferns

tree fern

3 x Astelia
chathamica
'Silver Spear'
with
interplanted
Nicotiana
sylvestris

tree fern

bananas

existing Escallonia *retained*
for screening from wind

The Diagnosis

This is a very unusual front garden: first because you leave the house and cross a public road to get to it, and second because it slopes so steeply, falling about 5m (15ft) over a distance of 12m (36ft) or so. The bottom of the garden ends in a sheer drop of about 2.4m (8ft) to the main road into town.

The top end of the garden was almost vertical in places, and had been cut into a series of terraces, with large shrubs such as buddleja, weigela, lonicera and rhododendrons providing a hedge at the very top of the bank. These plants also performed a far more important function in that they acted as a binding agent, with their roots holding the steeply sloping bank in place and reducing land slippage and soil erosion.

The middle section of the garden was dominated by a large eucalyptus which was looking rather the worse for wear, having been battered by high winds and pruned after a fashion. It may not have been the ideal specimen tree, but it was also acting to stabilize the soil bank in the top half of the garden. Below the tree, a sloping lawn ran through the next area of the garden before ending in a small curved border containing a range of interesting plants. The one which really caught our attention was a young *Crinodendron hookerianum* (Chilean lantern tree),

which is a good indicator of a fertile, well-drained acid soil.

The one thing that was glaringly obvious about this garden was that we could neither make the slope go away, nor change it to any great extent. So, quite early in the proceedings, we decided to turn it to our advantage by emphasizing the slope and making it a feature of the garden – in other words working with it, rather than against it – and constructing a wooden deck to link the different levels of the garden.

We also realized that we could use the mild climate found on this part of the Cornish peninsula to grow plants which would normally require protection in other parts of the country.

We felt that due to the close proximity of the sea (from the top of the garden you felt that you could reach over the bay and touch it), we should look at some nautical link, if possible. Some weathered or sea-washed timber could be included somewhere, to make furniture, steps or a platform of some kind. The uppermost section of the garden was much more exposed than the rest, as it received no benefit at all from the escallonia hedge which protected the lower two-thirds of the garden, though it received the most sunlight and was hot and dry so was ideal for sun-loving plants.

Of all the gardens covered to date, this one has the mildest climate and longest growing season, so we could use a much wider range of plants here. In some respects we felt spoilt for choice (not that we complained) about this particular advantage, one that most gardeners would give their eye teeth for.

Changes had to be made to the deck for safety reasons – there was a drop of 2m (6ft) from the top of the deck to the garden below, so we had to put up some form of safety rail. We mounted posts on the front edge of the deck, and rather than have a solid rail, we used a thick rope, threaded through the posts and pulled taut.

We were unable to obtain sufficient supplies of *Phyllostachys nigra* (black-stemmed bamboo) to form a hedge, and we replaced it with *Phormium tenax purpureum* (New Zealand flax).

Hard Landscaping

As with many other gardens, we started this one by deciding which plants were to be given a reprieve. We walked around the garden with Judy and marked the plants she wished to keep with red ribbon, to make sure they were not discarded by mistake. They were placed in pots and polythene bags to prevent them from drying out, and then taken up on to a small terraced area just in front of the house. As soon as we had saved the plants, the real work could start.

▲ *Judy and Ciarán's garden in the early stages of construction, showing the creation of the top terrace.*

We began by setting the levels and marking out the positions for the supporting posts and joists to hold the deck in position. Setting out and marking in this garden was far from easy, due to the steep slope, but it was essential to get it absolutely correct because of the amount of excavation work we were about to do. The deck consisted entirely of recycled timber, most of it from decommissioned fishing boats which were (sadly) being broken up about a mile away from where we were working. The posts were the only timber we actually bought, and we started by digging the holes for the posts which would form the main strengthening framework to the whole structure. When it was finished, this prominent feature provided an excellent position from which to survey the rest of the garden, and excellent views over the town and quay below.

The deck was the most dominant feature of the garden and would take up most of our time, so we started building it as soon as we could. The posts at the back of the deck (the highest point up the bank) were inserted 1m (3ft) deep into the bank, and concreted into position. At the front things were a little more complicated, because we had to 'cut and fill' the soil to achieve the required depth for the retaining wall and the front edge of the deck. This process involved chopping vertically into the bank to a depth of 1m (3ft) and clearing all the soil away. The topsoil was stacked to one side as we worked. The subsoil, once exposed, was dug away and spread at the lowest corners of the garden to bring up the levels, and once this had been firmed and roughly levelled, we spread the topsoil over it. We had to cut through a number of roots originating from the eucalyptus, but these were all carefully trimmed to encourage rapid healing and the formation of a branching root system just behind the cut. After the bank had been excavated, we inserted the front support posts 1m (3ft) deep into the bank and concreted them into position, leaving just over 2m (6ft) of post standing upright out of the soil.

These posts were all interconnected by fixing cross-members (joists) to them. As well as holding the whole frame together, these joists would act to support the decking boards. In order to prevent the central area of the deck from sagging, we put in a row of intermediate upright posts to provide extra strength. The deck boards, which consisted of wooden planks from the hold of a fishing boat, were then nailed onto the joists. On the second day, when the sun came out briefly, the upper section of the garden took on the gentle aroma of a fishmonger's, so we knew that the garden would at least be popular with the local cats.

Before we started work on the garden, Ciarán had been very busy – rebuilding a stone wall, arranging the supply of the ship's timbers, and building two flights of steps. The first flight ran from the road at the top of the garden down on to the deck, and the second flight (which he assembled while we were there) ran from the front of the deck down into the bottom section of the garden. We made the safety rail supports from thick rope, threaded through posts, to blend in with our nautical theme.

We used more ship's planking to form the retaining wall which held back the soil in front of the deck. These planks were cut to length and slotted into position behind the upright posts, from the base upwards. Each board was held in position by filling in soil behind it to push it firmly forward against the supporting posts, and in the area where the tree roots were, we incorporated some granular fertilizer to encourage root growth.

At the base of the retaining wall we introduced a water feature, consisting of an old plastic water cistern buried into the ground with its rim just above soil level. A piece of copper pipe positioned in the retaining wall providing a steady trickle of water into the cistern, where a hidden submersible pump circulated it back round the system. Initially, when we started the pump, we found that the water jet was just too strong, even on the lowest setting. The problem of slowing the water flow was eventually solved by closing off part of the water intake using a penny.

Soft Landscaping

This garden at first seemed a potential problem site with its precipitous slope, but after it had been terraced it was possible to see that it had several immediate advantages. The established eucalyptus provided the garden with a permanent and established atmosphere – once its trunk was emphasized by the decking it came into its own. The top terraces would provide a free-draining, sunny habitat for spiky architectural subjects, and the subsequent levelling of the lower area gave us a sheltered and moist area for exotic jungle-like plants.

Materials and equipment

Softwood posts, treated (20cm x 15cm
    diameter x 4m)
Postfixing cement (6 bags)
Slow-release fertilizer (35 x 80-litre bags)
Fine-grade mulch (12 x 80-litre bags)
Coarse-grade mulch (12 x 80-litre bags)
Wood preservative (5-litre can)
Glyphosate weedkiller (1-litre can)
Coil of 18mm nylon rope for bannisters
    (20-meter coil)
Terracotta pots (3 x 7.5-litre)
(All timber for decking boards and joists were
donated by local fishermen from boats which
were being broken up after decommissioning.)
Crowbar
Digging spades (10)
Garden forks (10)
Shovels (4)
Power drill
Extension cables (2 x 35-metre)
Pruning saw
Hack saw
Rip saw
Coil of 40mm polypropylene rope, orange for
    marking out (30-metre coil)

Water feature: Copper pipe (1m x 32mm)
Plastic hose (4m x 25mm)
Submersible pump (400 diamond series)
Car battery (12-volt)
Water tank, recycled (50-litre)

The rhododendron at the very top of the garden was severely pruned but left as a backdrop to the garden and as a screen from the road. Its roots also gave stability to the bank. It was underplanted with a hedge of evergreen *Pittisporum tobira*, which was continued around the top of the new stone wall to screen the garden completely and provide a scented welcome at the garden gate.

Two large clumps of dramatic bronze-leaved phormium were planted, one on either side of the gate, to mark the entrance and immediately provide a clue that this was an exotic garden. Phormiums are well known for their wind-tolerance, and as this was the most exposed situation in the garden they were ideal. Their strong fibrous roots would also help to bind the bank. On opening the gate, the garden

▲ *The garden as it will appear in its third year, brugmansia and tree ferns creating a sense of excitement by the steps and softening the construction.*

▼ *With the top terrace completed, work gets underway on the planting.*

▲ *The wooden terrace with pots of* **Agave americana variegata,** *plus an addition made by Judy and Ciarán themselves in the shape of half a boat, upturned and used as a seat, in keeping with the nautical theme of the terrace.*

would immediately present itself as an exotic retreat. Descending the steps, plants were positioned to overhang and interact with the visitor – billowing *Pittisporum tobira* to the right and the tree-fern *Cyathea dealbata*, with silvered undersides to the leaves, hovering above the steps. The giant architectural *Furcraea longaeva* was pushed into cracks to erupt at random from the steep bank. A datura was planted immediately beside the steps for its night-scented flowers and obviously exotic growth.

Once you were standing on the deck, the top terrace would reveal itself with spiky domes of *Dasylirion acrotrichum* and dense, solid mounds of *Agave celsii. Agave americana* was planted higher up,

to jut out above eye contact, and soft pennisetum grass and agapanthus were interplanted throughout to unite the terraces and give seasonal flowers and seedheads, softening the architectural foliage. At the top we planted the large-leaved *Tetrapanax papyrifera* against the shelter of the rhododendron. Breezes would catch the leaves and reveal soft felted undersides. The cracks of the wall were crammed with succulent aeoniums. The steps down into the lower garden were framed with three pot-grown variegated agaves to hold the eye. The pots would add a contrast to the wild planting below.

From the wooden decking of the top terrace the view into the garden below would highlight the giant cartwheels of the tree-fern and an exotic tapestry of foliage. The steps down into this area were planted with scented jasmine to scramble up the banister and partially screen out the neighbouring garden. The descent would once again be marked with a datura, nestled in the sheltered lee of the steps and the retaining wall to the terrace.

Three large tree-ferns were planted first, as the key plants for the lower garden. Clustered around the stone seat, they were placed on different levels so that they enclosed the seat and created a secret hideaway that would be quite private from above. In contrast to the initial view from the deck, the hideaway would allow views up through the foliage. A fourth tree-fern in the centre of the lower area would provide a visual link with the main grouping.

The gaps in the bottom hedge, which was retained as a vital windbreak, were filled out with the wind-tolerant evergreen *Arbutus unedo*, with bell-shaped autumn flowers followed by orange fruit. In front of the arbutus, two palms were planted – in the early years their exotic evergreen leaves would add a

shiny backdrop to the planting in front, and as they established they would rise above the garden with strong trunks and dense growth to echo the tree-ferns in the opposite corner.

A clump of phormium to tie in with those up by the entrance gate masked out the neighbouring garden without dominating the horizon. Working down through the collection of key plants we placed *Sparmannia africana* within the shelter of the stone wall. Normally used as a houseplant, it would need the wind protection to prevent its leaves being torn and tattered. The same applied to the bananas, which were placed in the most sheltered position of all at the base of the escallonia hedge – leaves with a large surface area are more prone to wind damage.

After the key plants had been placed we added

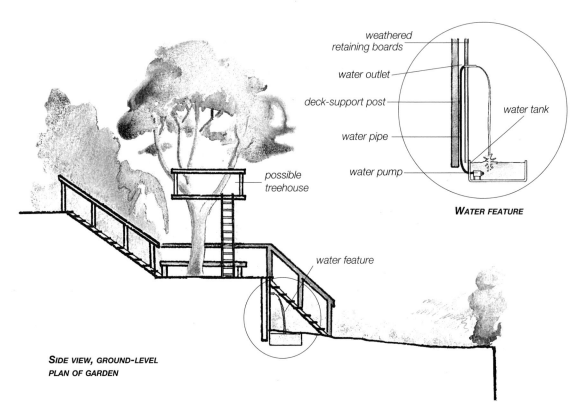

weathered
retaining boards

water outlet

deck-support post

water pipe

water pump

water tank

WATER FEATURE

possible
treehouse

water feature

**SIDE VIEW, GROUND-LEVEL
PLAN OF GARDEN**

the detail plants for contrast and filling out. The sweet-smelling ginger *Hedychium gardnerianum* was placed by the stone seat, and a large clump of papyrus was planted by the water trough. Its growth would arch over the water spout, helping to create a sense of mystery. Pinpricks of colour were introduced with an interplanting of fiery-red *Crocosmia* 'Lucifer'. This was repeated among the bananas with the crocosmia and leafy golden-flowered ligularia. *Crinum powellii* 'Album' was added underneath the datura to arch over the water from the other side, and the giant lily-like *Cardiocrinum giganteum* was secreted away underneath the tree-ferns.

The whole planting was united with a blanket planting of the rusty evergreen grass *Stipa arundinacea*. Another good plant for capturing the breeze, this would act as the base plant from which all the larger plants would emerge, creating a multi-layered jungle-like effect. Odd gaps and crevices were filled with rapid-growing echiums, *Nicotiana sylvestris* and *Geranium palmatum*. When the garden was established these would self-seed into any available gaps, and in the early years they would fill up the garden to help give the impression that it had always been there.

All the plants in the scheme were chosen for their exotic growth, although many of them are in fact quite hardy. Bold foliage and careful positioning highlighted the element of surprise. With the obvious advantages of the Cornish climate, the design was pushed to its limits, careful consideration being given to those corners in the garden which were sheltered from drying wind and cold.

As soon as the plants in the top terraces had been put in, they were given a top-dressing of granular fertilizer and a good watering, followed by a thick mulch of composted organic matter. The bulk of the

---

Plants and seeds

Aeonium cuneatum
Agapanthus 'Headbourne Hybrids'
Agave americana variegata
Agave celsii
Arbutus unedo
Astelia chathamica 'Silver Spear'
Brugmansia x *candida* 'Knightii'
Brugmansia suaveolens
Canna indiflora
Cardiocrinum giganteum
Crinum x *powellii* 'Album'
Crocosmia 'Lucifer'
Cyathea dealbata
Cyperus involucrata
Dasylirion acrotrichum
Dicksonia antarctica
Echium pininiana
Furcraea longaeva
Geranium palmatum
Hedychium gardnerianum
Ipomaea learii
Ligularia stenocephala 'The Rocket'
Musa basjoo
Nicotiana sylvestris
Pennisetum villosum
Phormium tenax 'Purpureum'
Pittisporum tenuifolium 'Purpureum'
Pittisporum tobira
Rheum palmatum 'Rubrum'
Sparmannia africana
Stipa arundinacea
Tetrapanax papyrifer
Trachycarpus fortunei
Woodwardia radicans
Zantedeschia aethiopica
Zantedeschia 'Aztec Gold'

---

planting in the lower section of the garden went very quickly once all the plants had been carried down into the garden and placed in position. We did not apply a mulch to this area, as all the plants were going into a

◀ *Rope salvaged from the boats in the nearby bay is used as a safety rail for the top terrace.*

▶ *Looking through the garden from the corner of the 'jungle' dell. Echiums provide instant lush growth just three months after planting. They will flower the following year and then die, seeding into new positions. In the early stages, their rapid growth covers far slower-growing subjects.*

▼ *Judy and Ciarán on the deck. The drystone walls planted with the rapid-growing echiums provide early interest while slower-growing subjects establish.*

mixture of half soil and half organic compost, but we did water everything thoroughly once it was in the ground.

In the pool we planted three pot-grown zantedeschia, and as these prefer to grow in shallow water, we placed the pots on stacks of bricks so that the crown of the plant was just 10cm (4in) below water level. In order to keep the water clear, a layer of gravel was placed over the compost in each pot to prevent the peat-based compost from floating out

and clouding the water too much.

In building this garden we were helped by a group of very enthusiastic and extremely competent students from the Duchy College of Horticulture. One of these students was an area supervisor for the local authority parks department, and he was able to provide us with a massive unwanted specimen of *Phormium tenax* 'Purpureum' from the local park, which we were able to dig up and divide before taking it back to the site for planting.

Herne Hill

A Vertical Garden
Herne Hill, London

The Client

This four-storey mansion block of eight flats, like many others in London and other large cities, is functional but rather nondescript and certainly not eye-catching. The rear of the building looks out over a small communal garden, and over rooftops with television antennae sticking up into the skyline rather than the trees that most residents would prefer to see. From outside, looking towards the back of the building, its appearance is dominated by a superstructure of black-painted metal fire escapes and balconies to every floor.

The occupants have varied and interesting backgrounds and lifestyles, and their ages range right across the demographic spectrum. An interest in gardening already existed when we became involved, because a number of the residents are allotment holders who travel considerable distances to tend their plots.

The group were keen to utilize the balconies at the rear of the property and saw them as an opportunity to create a social space in the summer. Several people had already made a start with pot-grown plants in the previous summer, but the exposed situation and lack of knowledge meant that their success to date had been limited. They talked about the hanging gardens on balconies in Barcelona and parts of France, and were keen to create a feeling of abundance and greenery.

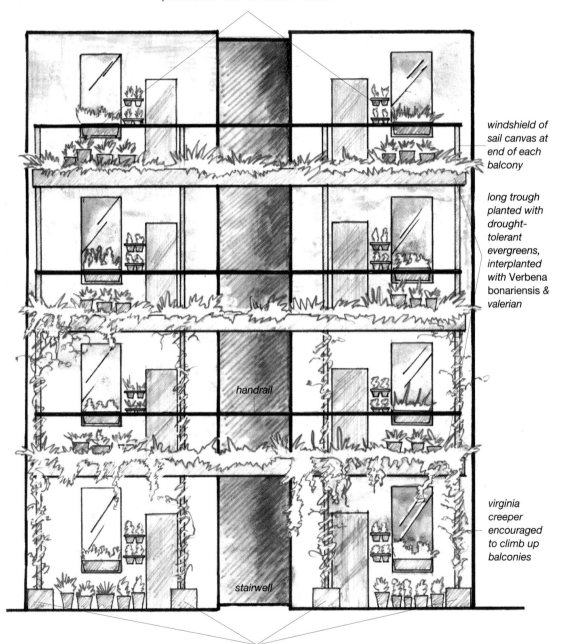

wall-mounted pots & window boxes
planted with each flat-owner's choice

windshield of
sail canvas at
end of each
balcony

long trough
planted with
drought-
tolerant
evergreens,
interplanted
with Verbena
bonariensis &
valerian

handrail

virginia
creeper
encouraged
to climb up
balconies

stairwell

troughs constructed around concrete
pilings planted with climbers

▲ *Herne Hill, south London: soon this small mansion block will be transformed into a vertical oasis of greenery against the concrete lines of London's urban landscape.*

▼ *The residents discuss their various ideas before planting begins.*

Shelagh, at ground level, had already started gardening in pots. She was quite sure what she wanted and drew up a list of plants from each astrological sign for their medicinal and healing properties. Denise, by contrast, wanted containers full of colourful annuals and tender perennials that she could change throughout the year.

On the first level, Claire wanted a mix of herbs and flowers. She was keen to have sea-holly and plants which her daughter Colette could grow from seed. On the second level there was a definite desire to grow vegetables and herbs – Dave and Tim had an allotment and were keen to put their gardening experience to use on the balconies. They had grown sunflowers and honeysuckle the year before. Isabelle had a passion-flower which needed help, and she also wanted herbs for the kitchen.

The top level presented problems with increased exposure. Angela wanted strong, saturated colour and the chance to grow a rose. Rebecca and Paul were open-minded and keen to try anything that would succeed in the prevailing conditions.

Almost everyone in the block became interested in the project as it progressed, and they each became as involved in their own way as their time and work commitments allowed. The members of the group seemed to be used to helping one another in a

neighbourly way and were quite comfortable working together.

The Diagnosis

Gardening under the circumstances found at this site is certainly a challenge. The conditions range from very hot in the summer (especially in a city environment, where heat is reflected back off the walls) to cold in the winter, with the roots as well as the tops of the plants being subject to possible damage by the cold. A constant problem at this height would be wind exposure, which damages the plants, reduces growth rates and speeds up the drying-out process. In addition, whatever design option was chosen, we had the difficulties of limited access. As the balconies were only approximately 1m (3ft) wide, all the plants and materials would have to be carried up and down the fire escapes, which were just marginally wider at approximately 1.2m (4ft). It was obvious to us that unless we used either a 'cherry picker' or scaffolding (or both), we could only work from the balcony out over the troughs, which was not as safe as we would have liked.

The range of plants able to survive in these conditions was limited, especially as our aim was to try to have something in leaf at all times of the year. We had already realized that the building would look at its most drab in winter. Although most residents thought that the idea of the 'hanging gardens of Herne Hill' was a good one, they still wanted the freedom to grow a few plants of their choice, be it flowers or vegetables. In fact, many of them wanted to know just how many more edible plants they could grow in addition to those they had already tried. The residents on the ground floor were delighted that we were able to provide some planting containers for them, even though they did not have the balcony our brief was originally intended to cover.

Once we had fully analysed the situation, it was possible to give all interested parties a little of what they wanted, knowing that they possessed the enthusiasm to make it work. Even those who were not experienced gardeners were keen to try out ideas, and admitted that the building definitely needed something to cheer it up.

Many of the problems faced here were of an engineering and structural nature rather than those which gardeners would normally face. We had to have the plant troughs hung on the outside of the balconies, because the balconies were also fire escapes and placing troughs inside them would limit access and so infringe fire regulations. Due to the potential weight problems, tests had to carried out on the structural strength of these fire escapes, to

calculate a safe load-bearing capacity. This limited our options regarding the choice of compost, drainage material and watering system.

There is a natural assumption that if you are working on a vertical plane, the easiest thing to do is select trailing plants. However, we could not use long trailing plants here because of the high risk of wind damage, so we worked at convincing people that it was far better to use climbing plants, which would climb up if they had the support of the structure, particularly the handrail.

The only things that we really could not find a way round were in the ground-floor area, where we had to abandon a planting site because it would have restricted an access point too much, and we were unable to provide an automatic watering system for the individual pots and containers on the balcony, because the water running down the walls of the

building on a long-term basis may have caused some structural damage.

Hard Landscaping

Much of the hard-landscaping work had been done well in advance of the construction and planting stages. The metal troughs we prefabricated into a series of approximately 3m (10ft) sections, which took some manoeuvring into position. These troughs fitted snugly into a metal cage slung on the side of each balcony, painted black to blend in with the balconies and fire escapes on the building. Each trough tilted slightly (a fall of 1 in 300) towards one end, and at the lower end a drainage device was fitted to enable us to control the water level within the bottom of the trough, so that hopefully the containers should never be totally dry. The drainage device protruded up 4cm (1½in) above the base of the container, so drainage could only occur when the water level exceeded the top of the pipe.

The speed and frequency of the wind concerned us greatly, and in an attempt to combat this we attached canvas squares to the windward end of the balcony to provide some shelter. This did not protect

PLANT TROUGH (CROSS SECTION)

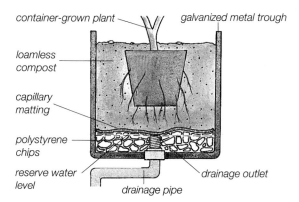

container-grown plant — galvanized metal trough

loamless compost

capillary matting

polystyrene chips

reserve water level

drainage outlet

drainage pipe

the planting troughs but it did help to protect the plants grown by the residents on the balcony itself.

In order to provide a suitable rooting environment, but at the same time being fully aware of the limitations on weight of the materials we could use, we prepared the troughs by pouring a layer of polystyrene chips into the base of each trough, levelling them out at a depth of 4cm (1½in), the same depth as the drainage device. This was a substitute for gravel to prevent the bottom of the containers getting too waterlogged. We covered this layer with a layer of capillary matting because it was porous and it stopped the compost mixing with the polystyrene and clogging the drainage system. Finally we poured in bags of peat-free, loamless compost before planting into this top layer.

After planting, we also installed an automatic watering system to keep the plants watered on a consistent and regular basis, rather than relying on each resident being responsible for a particular section of trough. Each floor could be isolated from the others, should the need arise. We used several different types of irrigation on the troughs, but the system chosen for the top balcony was the one which was capable of delivering the most water, as it was the most exposed level and we expected it to dry out the most rapidly.

For the ground-floor residents, we constructed some square boxes 60cm (2ft) deep by 1m (3ft), to fit around the base of each of the upright posts which supported the balconies. These were filled with compost and planted with climbers to be trained up the posts and create an instant impact.

When we were preparing to start on this site we found that it was impossible (and unsafe) to work from the balcony alone. We had to call in contractors and have scaffolding erected up the entire height of

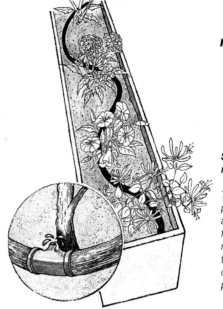

SEEP-HOSE IRRIGATION

The irrigation pipe is laid in a serpentine fashion with a nozzle close to the hose of each plant.

the building for safety reasons and to make it possible to complete the construction and planting of the troughs hanging from the balconies.

Soft Landscaping

The potential for gardening in containers is rarely exploited to its limits. This Herne Hill mansion block presented itself as an opportunity to clothe the face of

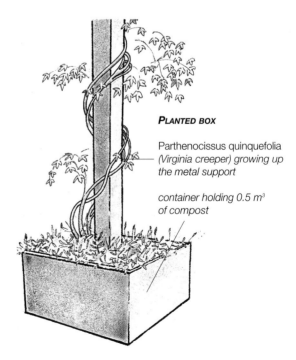

PLANTED BOX

Parthenocissus quinquefolia (Virginia creeper) growing up the metal support

container holding 0.5 m³ of compost

▲ *Dan and the residents planting the troughs along the balconies.*

◄ *The planting will grow out and soften the building in later years. Evergreens will provide constant interest when the Virginia creeper is dormant.*

▶ *Parthenocissus quinquefolia climbing up the balcony. With time it will cover the metalwork and form a curtain of greenery.*

Materials and equipment

Troughs (6)
Window boxes (8)
Secure plant hangers (40)
Empty oil-cans as containers (32 x 20 litres)
Terracotta pots (64 x 15cm/6in)
Canvas shields with eyelets (6)
New Horizons growing medium
   (40 x 80-litre bags)
Marine ply for ground-floor tubs
Peat-free loamless compost
   (100 x 80-litre bags)
Peat-based compost (50 x 80-litre bags)
Poly chips (15cu ft)
Capillary matting (60cm x 49m/2ft x 162ft)
Irrigation system
Hammerite paints (8 x 500ml)

---

a building with foliage and also within the scheme, in the area of each flat, to give the individual members an opportunity to express themselves.

Without any soil in sight, the scheme had to pay very careful consideration to the maintenance aspects of container gardening. Containers would have to be large enough to provide plants with adequate root space and a decent soil volume for a good moisture reservoir. The automatic watering system was attached to the communal trough running along the outside of the balconies.

One of the few places in which plants grow vertically in nature is on a cliff face. The planting was designed to mimic the way in which plants colonize a vertical face, seeding down from one level to the next. To unite the three troughs visually, a limited range of shrubs was chosen. These would be repeated from one level to the next so that from a distance there would be a continuity over the entire façade of the building. The choice of plants was limited to tough evergreens which could cope with exposure, both

from wind and sun, which was progressively more intense the higher the flat. *Senecio* 'Sunshine' and lavender formed the main silver element to the scheme. They would billow out and down and push through the railings. The forms would be round and solid and resistant to wind damage. This theme was taken through with the prostrate *Ceanothus thyrsiflorus* 'Repens' which would hang down to cover the trough and provide a dark accent and brilliant blue flowers early in the season.

Two climbers were given positions in the troughs. They would be encouraged into the railing to provide some screening on the balconies and to trail down and soften the lines of the separate levels. The semi-evergreen *Lonicera japonica* 'Halliana' was placed on two levels, with a large group of the blue-flowered potato vine, *Solanum crispum* 'Glasnevin', which without support tends to form a thicket of growth ideal for these conditions. A weeping *Buddleja alternifolia* was planted on the top level to cascade downward, and Virginia creeper and white potato vine were placed in the large planters at the base of each support, eventually to be trained up from one level to the next and to cascade down in a curtain of foliage. To soften the shrubby planting and provide a seasonal fluctuation of interest, *Verbena bonariensis* and the cliff-growing valerian were added in places. They would be left to seed from one area to the next.

The individual gardens attached to each flat were limited to a small group of containers. Each member was given the opportunity to express his or her likes and preferences, and then a selection was put together that would be appropriate to each flat. We used varieties such as the drought-tolerant blue-green grass *Festuca glauca* and *Convolvulus cneorum* on the top levels, and a *Rosa* 'Louis XIV' for its recurrent flowering and endurance as a containerized rose. Compact agapanthus and osteospermums were used for the same reasons.

On lower levels, where the exposure was less severe, we planted herbs in containers, drought-tolerant plants which become better for living in harsh conditions. On the second level Isabelle was keen to plant a passion-flower and a bay. These were given the largest containers and put in the lee of the canvas windshield we had placed at the end of the balcony.

On the first level Claire was given the exotic *Datura meteloides*, which was also placed in a sheltered corner, and sea holly which was planted both in the trough and in smaller containers to test its preference. As it is a tap rooter we felt it would be best in a good depth of soil. On the ground floor, where weight was not an issue and shelter was greater, a selection of herbs and annuals was put together to suit both flat members.

Most of the plants for this 'garden' were container-grown, and to be sure they would not dry out while being planted, we started the day by watering them. This meant that they were drained by the time we came to carry them, making them lighter and easier to handle.

The planting process started with the hard work of carrying all of the plants we required up to each floor, and standing them on the balcony. A great deal of this fetching and carrying was done by the residents, who laid out the plants on the ground in groups depending on which balcony they were destined for, so that the occupants of each floor could take the plants up to their own balcony. This was very useful as it helped us to check that we had actually received all the plants we had ordered. It also allowed us to space out the plants in their respective positions along the balcony as a dummy run before planting them into the troughs.

Once we had done this, we were in a position to start planting. To do this, we worked in pairs, with one person positioned on the balcony passing the plants over to their partner on the scaffolding boards, who could then plant them into the trough. We poured a layer of compost into the trough before planting started at the correct level for the root size of the largest plants.

It always helps to work to a set plan when planting, and between us we evolved a system. The largest specimens were planted first, then more compost was added and the next size of plant inserted, and so on until all the plants were in position. The troughs were then filled with compost to the rim, because we knew the compost would settle once it was watered and leave about 5cm (2in) of the rim showing.

The boxes we constructed for the ground-floor residents around the base of each of the upright support posts of the building were filled with compost and planted with climbers and shrubs. The 3m (10ft) high parthenocissus going in as specimen plants had to be trained up the posts and fanned out along the handrail of the first balcony. Hopefully when these plants come into leaf they will create an instant impact.

Once the planting had been finished, we tested the automatic irrigation system, and several of us were able to vouch (quite forcefully) for the fact that the system was working all too well in some places. Having said this, it is always better to check the system to be sure just how well the joints are connected and to determine whether or not there are any blockages.

Plants and seeds

Buddleja alternifolia
Ceanothus thyrsiflorus
  '*Repens*'
Centranthus ruber
Convolvulus cneorum
Erigeron karvinskianus
  '*Profusion*'
Euphorbia characias
Helichrysum serotinum
Ipomoea indica
Lavandula angustifolia
  '*Vera*'
Lonicera japonica
  '*Repens*'
Parthenocissus
  quinquefolia
Senecio '*Sunshine*'
Solanum crispum
  '*Glasnevin*'
Solanum jasminoides
  '*Album*'
Verbena bonariensis
Vitus vinifera '*Purpurea*'

PAUL & REBECCA: LEVEL 3
Festuca glauca
Lonicera japonica
  '*Halliana*'
Osteospermum '*Whirlygig*'
Surfinia petunias
  '*Dark Purple*'
Tomato '*Gardeners
  Delight*'

ANGELA, RAY & KHALID: LEVEL 3
Agapanthus campanulatus
  '*Iris*'
Chillies
Diascia rigescens
Lobelia '*Crystal Palace*'
Rosa '*Louis XIV*'

Neil, Tim, Dave & Isabelle: Level 2
Aloysia triphylla
Chives
Laurus nobilis (bay)
Passiflora caerulea
Rosmarinus officinalis

Tagetes '*Paprica*'
Tomato '*Golden Sunrise*'
Trailing French
  pelargoniums

CLAIRE & COLETTE: LEVEL 1
Eryngium tripartitum
Papaver nudicaule
Thymus '*Golden Queen*'
Tomato Sweet One
  Hundred

DENISE: GROUND LEVEL
Helichrysum petiolare
  '*Goring Silver*'
Helichrysum petiolare
  '*Limelight*'
Papaver nudicaule
Nicotiana '*Sensation
  Mixed*'
Pelargonium '*Scarlet
  Single*'
Surfinia petunias, blue
Surfinia petunias, pink

SHELAGH: GROUND LEVEL
Bronze fennel
Common sage
Marjoram
Rosa rubiginosa
Ruta graveolens
  '*Jackmans Blue*'
Sorrel
Thymus '*Golden Queen*'
Verbascum '*Helen
  Johnson*'

SEEDS
Cerinthe major
Common basil
Datura meteloides
Eschscholzia, mixed
Lettuce, oak-leaved
Nasturtium '*Dwarf Mixed*'
Night-scented stock
Parsley, curled
Ruby chard
Saladini (cut and
  come again)

▲ *(Left)* **Parthenocissus** *and* **Ceanothus.**

▲ *(Right) The space along the balconies becomes more pleasantly usable with the addition of foliage.*

▶ *Trailing petunias and* **Lobelia** *'Crystal Palace' in the containers.*

◀ **Lavandula augustifolia** *'Vera' and* **Erigeron Karvinskianus** *'Profusion' in troughs with* **Parthenocissus** *and* **Solanum** *to climb up the supports.*

▼ *Planting the convolvulus in the troughs.*

WXD Restaurant

A Modern Potager
Crouch End, London

The Client

The clients for this garden were a group of people (Danny, Eileen and Roz) who have put together a proposal for a new restaurant in this area of north London. They all have experience in catering and catering management, and this venture is seen as an expansion of their interests. The site chosen for the venture is an old, single-storey railway building which has been used for a number of purposes, such as mini-cab offices. The shell of the building appeared to be structurally sound, but the internal walls were to be removed or resited, to provide a suitable seating space.

The general feeling was that the triangular garden should be a spill-over from the restaurant, becoming a place to eat and sit out in the summer; again, a green oasis in a city environment. Keith, the architect, was keen to open up the whole of the wall running along the length of the garden and replace the wall with large glass doors so that there would be a feeling of the building merging into the garden and vice versa. He was keen to keep the whole development as clean and as minimal as possible.

Danny, by contrast, wanted the whole space to be vibrant and lively – he wanted masses of colour and excitement and an almost continental atmosphere which would reflect the eclectic ethos of his

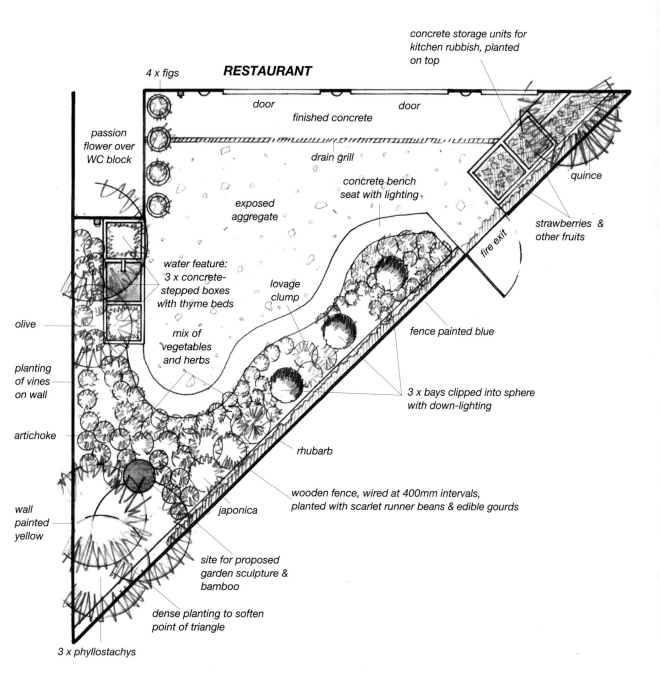

concrete storage units for
kitchen rubbish, planted
on top

4 x figs

RESTAURANT

door

finished concrete

door

passion
flower over
WC block

drain grill

concrete bench
seat with lighting

exposed
aggregate

quince

strawberries &
other fruits

water feature:
3 x concrete-
stepped boxes
with thyme beds

lovage
clump

fire exit

fence painted blue

olive

mix of
vegetables
and herbs

planting
of vines
on wall

3 x bays clipped into sphere
with down-lighting

artichoke

rhubarb

wall
painted
yellow

japonica

wooden fence, wired at 400mm intervals,
planted with scarlet runner beans & edible gourds

site for proposed
garden sculpture &
bamboo

dense planting to soften
point of triangle

3 x phyllostachys

restaurants in general. He wanted the garden to have
a 'wow' factor which could be seen from the street.
It needed to be an attraction for his customers and
something which would set the restaurant apart
from others.

Roz and Eileen were the gardening interest in the
team. They wanted an eclectic mix of plants which
could be used in the kitchen – herbs, vegetables and
fruit. They wanted the garden to feel exotic and
abundant – a place where they could potter around
and tend plants when they weren't working in the
restaurant itself.

Everyone thought that the garden should go
beyond the boundaries of what would normally be
expected of restaurant gardens. It should be usable
during the day and by night, and it should also be fun,
exciting and unexpected.

The Diagnosis

When we first saw this site, the vegetation consisted
almost entirely of *Buddleja davidii* ranging from 2m to
2.5m (6 to 8ft) in height. It was impossible to see from
one end of the small garden to the other, and the only
thing that stopped the light being blocked out
completely was the fact that it was winter and the
plants had no leaves on them. We could only get a
good look at the garden from the roof of a nearby

building, and it proved to be roughly triangular in shape and really quite small. On one side it was bounded by the wall of a two-storey building, which gets very warm during the early part of the day. The boundary on the longest side of the wall consists of a low wall about 1m (3ft) high, with a wooden-slatted fence of about 2m (6ft) high on top of it. The third side of the triangle is the building which will house the new restaurant.

The first aim was to make a garden where all the plants would be safe (not poisonous or an irritant to the skin) and preferably edible, with the common theme that all or part of most of them could be used for food if necessary (though it was never intended to try to supply the restaurant with food in the way that you would from a vegetable garden). Because this was a commercial venture, the second aim was to create a light relaxing atmosphere which would encourage the clientele to stay in the garden to enjoy a meal and a drink. What was needed was something that would make the area look larger than it actually was, and so the idea grew of a serpentine wall as a seat running around the garden, leading the eye, the wavy line giving the impression of covering a far greater distance than in reality. Keeping this wall quite low, about 50cm (20in), with tall plants growing around the perimeter of the garden, would help to

create an enclosed and safe feeling. As the garden was to be used in the evening as well as in the day, garden lighting was also suggested.

The range of plants we were able to suggest for this garden was greater than you could normally expect to grow at this latitude, because built-up areas such as London tend to have their own microclimate, and are often several degrees warmer than the surrounding countryside.

The main constraints with this project were things which were always beyond our control as a landscape team: problems with construction and conversion work within the building itself, late delivery of building materials, and limited availability of some group members, due mainly to other commitments. Compromises had to be made because of health and safety regulations – we had to change part of the layout to make room for a fire escape from the building out through the garden.

Hard Landscaping

The work started with the clearance and removal of the very well-established buddleja plants which had colonized the whole area. During this process, while the ground was being cleared and cultivated, several unexpected discoveries were made. We uncovered parts of old refrigerators, rotting galvanized steel

▲ **The WXD site before the hard landscaping is laid down.**

buckets, and the usual plethora of debris (a liberal sprinkling of soft drinks containers, polystyrene cups and cartons, newspapers and assorted food wrappers). In addition, we unearthed bits of paving slabs, bricks, and pieces of half-rotted wood in various shapes and sizes.

These discoveries make you appreciate just how resilient *Buddleja davidii* really is. As work progressed and we gradually found soil, we started to realize that we did have some raw material in which to grow plants. After the ground had been cleared, the site was back in the hands of the builders for the next stage of the construction work.

On our next visit the garden looked smaller than ever for a while, as the low serpentine wall had been cast in concrete, and a large part of the garden was occupied by the shuttering which held the concrete in position until it had set. The highest wall had been painted mustard-yellow, which reflected the sun's rays brilliantly and made the half of the garden nearest the wall seem much warmer already. We re-painted the slatted fence, changing it from a dark matt brown into a stunning peacock-blue which gave the whole garden a lift. Once the paint had dried, we drilled the wall and the fence to insert vine eyes so that we could string galvanized wires along the fence and wall. The wires were essential to provide support for the climbers we were going to use to cover the fence and take the blank appearance off the wall.

We then started on the garden by carefully removing the wooden shuttering to reveal the new concrete wall beneath, leaving the middle section in place to protect the relatively soft concrete for as long as we could. The next task was to wheelbarrow in several cubic metres of topsoil to raise the levels behind the concrete wall before we could do any planting. All of this topsoil had to be transported from the road outside, through the partially renovated building, over the concrete wall (this is why we left some shuttering in place), and into the area which would eventually become planted borders. As the soil was brought into the garden, we spread and levelled it to make borders mixing it with organic matter to encourage good root growth.

To one side of the garden, we built a water feature, consisting of a series of concrete box-sections stacked on top of each other to form troughs. These were cemented together, and the one which we intended to use as a small pool was painted on the inside with pond sealant to enable it to hold water. A submersible pump was placed in the bottom of this 'pool', and a water supply was routed through the adjoining container to create a slow-flow water jet which would gently trickle into the pool. This would provide some sound and movement in the garden, as well as raising the humidity of the warmest area close to the wall. The troughs not used for the water feature will be ideal for filling with culinary herbs, which can be picked for use in the kitchen with a minimum of effort, and are quickly and easily accessible.

All this development continued even though the floor for the hard-surface area of the garden had not been constructed, and there was still a considerable amount of construction work going on inside the building as well as out in the garden.

Soft Landscaping

The confines of this triangular garden needed to be softened by a dense planting. First, the apex of the triangle was disguised with a large and lush-growing group of golden-stemmed bamboo. This would be a continual presence in the garden all year round – its growth would reach the top of the fence and fill out to relieve the awkwardness of the corner. It would also provide a good foil for sculpture and a framework for uplighting, which would cast shadows on to the tall wall. The rustle of its leaves in the garden would create a sense of calm. We planted it in a good depth of soil, mulching it with a 10cm (4in) layer of organic matter to conserve moisture in the early years. The tall south-facing wall would quite literally heat the garden up and dry the plants out faster than usual, so care was taken when planting to ensure that adequate moisture-retaining humus was introduced into the soil.

As the garden needed to look good all the year round, it was important that it had a strong framework of evergreens through which seasonal

---

Materials and equipment

Submersible pump
Copper piping (18 x 1½in) 1 length
Morph spotlights (9)
Nimbus recessed uplighters (3)
Paint: Betty Blue 2 (2.5 litres)
Paint: Imperial Chinese Yellow (8 litres)
Paint: Persian Peacock – flat oil (8 litres)
Galvanized wire for cordons (50m/164ft)
Eyed bolts for cordon wire (60)
Irrigation system (leaky and drip hoses,
    connectors, timer switch)
4 Terracotta pots (19½in)
Mix 'N' Mulch (30 x 80 litres)
Aquaseal 40 (1 gallon)
Topsoil (4cu m)

---

perennials and vegetables could intermingle. The next key plant to be positioned, against the sunny wall, was a young olive. In the microclimate of London, olives are quite hardy and have even been known to fruit. This plant would be encouraged to fill the corner and arch over the small water feature. In its shelter in the very warmest corner we planted a lemon, using the variety 'Meyer', which has been grown with some success in the shelter of warm walls. This was obviously pushing the garden's microclimate to its limits, but with a little protection such as straw around its trunk or fleece in the coldest weather, the lemon was worth a try.

The last shrubby evergreens planted to make a link to the bamboo were a small group of loquat, *Eriobotrya japonica*. Three plants were planted close together, to give the impression of one multi-stemmed plant. This is a good device when a bushy shrub is required in a short space of time. The garden

◀ *The mix of evergreens and annuals will provide constant interest in the small confines of this garden and will soften the hard and prominent boundaries.*
▶ *The garden in its early stages. The restaurant is open, although the building works are still not quite completed. Phyllostachys aurea in the foreground is used to soften the point of the triangle. Clipped spheres of bay are focal points in the main bed.*
▼ *Removing the framework for the concrete curving wall.*

needed to look established quickly, and it was important that there was an immediate impact.

Three spherical bay trees gave an instant presence and order to the eclectic planting. Once the main feature plants were in, the climbers could be placed at the back of the beds to mask the fence and the walls. Both surfaces were covered with grape vines, a variety which tastes of strawberries – vines love a hot dry site and with their rampant growth would take the green of the garden vertically upwards. On the fence the vine was combined with the golden hop for its bright splash of foliage, and with runner beans and gourds.

In the corner by the lemon, in the hottest part of the garden, a passion-flower was planted so it would scramble over the toilet block to soften that part of the building. By the fire exit we planted two kiwi fruits, a male and a female for cross-pollination. These

would be trained back towards the building.

After the climbers had been planted and their young growths wired in, the evergreen shrubs were added: a drift of aromatic purple sage right along the curve of bed as a year-round solid front to the border. Plants of rosemary, 'Miss Jessop's Upright', were interplanted behind the concrete containers to capitalize on the sunshine and fill an awkward space with continual interest. The rosemary would also be a soft foil for the planting in the containers in front.

When the framework plants were in, the next stage was to plant groups of perennials, allowing gaps between them for annual herbs and vegetables. Towards the back we planted lovage for its tall elegant growth and leaf, and rhubarb in the shade of the loquat. Around the bamboo a large clump of bronze fennel was placed as a dark foil for the silver-leaved globe artichokes in front. The architectural leaves of the artichoke would provide drama and the fennel soft contrast.

Physalis franchettii, the Cape gooseberry, was planted along the front of the dark bay trees to make a contrast with its red lantern-shaped fruit, and feathery asparagus was planted between. The gaps between would be filled with oak-leaved lettuce and ruby chard for their excellent foliage, and interplanted leeks would be allowed to seed and add a vertical accent. Edible flowers such as marigolds and nasturtiums would be grown in drifts, and tomatoes would be squeezed in along the sunny wall and trained up tall hazel canes. The pond was planted with the beautiful-leaved arrowhead.

The concrete container by the bench was filled with a flat planting of thyme and a mix of brilliant red-leaved basil and parsley was planted in the other. Some large terracotta pots were placed outside the door, and were planted with figs, a quince and strawberries. The figs fruit best in cramped root conditions, and their leaves would add a Mediterranean air. Vegetables and herbs could continue to be added in the gaps left between the perennial planting – above all, the planting was designed to be relaxed, lighthearted and fun.

Much of the soil in the garden was in a very sorry state, contaminated as it was with fragments of broken glass, cement, brick and rusting metal. There was very little trace of organic matter and hardly any signs of worm activity. Obviously this had to be rectified, and we added about 60cm (2ft) of imported topsoil on to this existing layer.

To prepare this new soil, generous amounts of fertilizer and organic compost were added in an attempt to promote the rapid establishment of the new plants. This was added as a covering to the new soil and dug in to a full fork's depth. Mixing the soil and compost to this depth encourages the plants to root deeply, which is very important in a dry, hot garden such as this one.

All the larger plants used in this garden were grown in containers, and we did not tease out the roots when we planted as we wanted to minimize root disturbance. We found that a number of pots

▼ **At work in the kitchen: WXD serves its first dishes on opening night.**

Plants and seeds

Actinidia chinensis (male
   and female)
Allium cepa (Egyptian onion)
Angelica archangelica
Artichoke
Asparagus 'Connovers Colossal'
Bronze fennel
Citrus x meyeri 'Meyer'
Cydonia oblonga 'Vranja' (quince)
Eriobotrya japonica (loquat)
Ficus carica (fig)
Humulus lupulus 'Aureus'
Laurus nobilis (bay)
Lovage
Olea europaea
Passiflora caerulea
Phyllostachys aurea

Physalis franchettii
Rhubarb 'Timperley Early'
Rosmarinus officinalis 'Miss
   Jessop's Upright'
Rubus calycinoides 'Emerald
   Carpet'
Sagittaria sagittifolia
Salvia officinalis 'Purpurescens'
Sorrel
Strawberry
Thymus 'Porlock'
Thymus 'Silver Posie'
Vitis vinifera 'Purpurea'

SEEDS
Basil 'Dark Opal'
Bean 'Scarlet Runner'

Calabrese, purple sprouting
Chilli
Coriander 'Celantro'
Gourds (special mix ornamental)
Helianthus 'Sunbeam'
Leek
Lettuce, oak-leaved
Nasturtium (mixed bush)
Nasturtium (mixed trailing)
Orach, red
Origanum vulgare
Parsley, curled
Ruby chard
Pot marigold
Tomato 'Golden Sunrise'
Tomato 'Tigrida'

were quite dry when they were delivered (one of the golden-stemmed bamboos was actually flagging), and these were soaked in a bucket of water until the rootball was thoroughly wet. A generous handful of general fertilizer was scattered around each plant when it was firmed into position, and each was given a good watering. After planting, a 5cm (2in) mulch of organic matter was applied over the soil to reduce water loss and prevent weed seeds germinating. As soon as all the planting and mulching had been finished, a slow-running hose was used to thoroughly soak the mulch and the soil beneath.

◀ Strawberries were planted around potted figs used to soften the rendered wall.

▶ The garden three months after planting. The evergreens provide structure while the annuals and climbers are establishing themselves. Lighting will transform the garden by night and extend its use considerably as the garden develops.

▼ A view of the restaurant from inside during the evening, looking out into the garden beyond.

Meri and Dick

A Shade Garden
Berkshire

The Client

Meri and Dick live in a semi-detached house in a quiet road, situated on a late-1960s estate at the edge of a village near Newbury in Berkshire. They have three children, whose ages range from teenage down to one year old. Dick is an engineer; he enjoys building things in the garden and is interested in plants, but does not consider himself to be a gardener. Meri, who comes from the United States, was already a keen and knowledgeable gardener and had attended classes in horticulture.

Meri said that on her first visit to the house she walked straight through the building to marvel at the woodland beyond. She feels a strong affinity with the trees and was keen that the garden should blend as much as possible with the woodland beyond its rigid boundaries. She had a well-developed sense of taste and a good idea of the limitations of the dry and overcast site. She had discovered that white flowers gave an extra half an hour of interest at the end of the day and had decided to include many plants which would show up in shady conditions.

Between them Meri and Dick had already set up a sound working garden, with a play area for the children, bold wooden swings and naturalistic planting. They wanted a hard surface immediately outside the house as a spillover from the dining-room, and an area of lawn for the

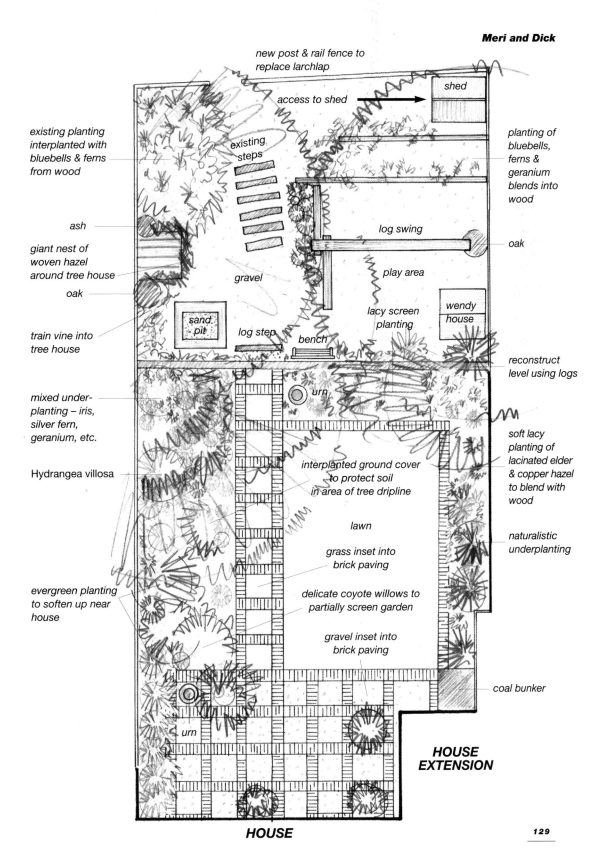

new post & rail fence to
replace larchlap

access to shed

shed

existing planting
interplanted with
bluebells & ferns
from wood

existing
steps

planting of
bluebells,
ferns &
geranium
blends into
wood

ash

log swing

oak

giant nest of
woven hazel
around tree house

gravel

oak

play area

train vine into
tree house

sand
pit

log step

bench

lacy screen
planting

wendy
house

reconstruct
level using logs

urn

mixed under-
planting – iris,
silver fern,
geranium, etc.

soft lacy
planting of
lacinated elder
& copper hazel
to blend with
wood

Hydrangea villosa

interplanted ground cover
to protect soil
in area of tree dripline

lawn

naturalistic
underplanting

grass inset into
brick paving

evergreen planting
to soften up near
house

delicate coyote willows to
partially screen garden

gravel inset into
brick paving

coal bunker

urn

HOUSE
EXTENSION

HOUSE

▲ The formal boundaries of Meri and Dick's garden were naturally blended with the woodland beyond.
▼ Meri, Dick and their children amongst the ferns, iris and sweet woodruff at the bottom of the garden.

children. The younger members of the family would definitely be included in the new scheme.

Daunted by years of trial and error, Meri felt she wanted a new start and was not averse to the main body of the garden being altered so that it would work with the existing conditions and not fight against them. She had a love of woodland plants which she was keen to pursue, and wanted the garden to be an escape from the house – a place for summer living with the family.

The Diagnosis

This long narrow garden has a beautiful setting, with three mature oak trees and the bottom end of the garden falling away to a backdrop of woodland just over the boundary fence. However, this setting also has its problems. The trees cause a considerable amount of shade when they are in leaf, and, to make the situation worse, they have a large root-spread which not only restricts cultivation but also dries out the soil, making life virtually impossible for anything planted beneath them. In this particular environment, the competition for water, nutrients and light must have been very intense during the recent dry summers. The soil was very stony, looking a bit like a gravel-pit with a sprinkling of soil – although the soil, surprisingly (especially in the lawn area), was very

poorly drained. We found that this was due to a 'pan' – a hard, compacted layer about 10cm (4in) below the surface, which impeded drainage and was a contributory factor to the thin, sparse growth of the lawn.

Possibly the most difficult environment in which to grow plants is dry shade, where the plants concerned face a constant struggle to obtain enough water and light. The size of the garden was also a major factor, as we would not be able to introduce earth-moving machinery because of lack of access; the play area, however, was actually quite well laid out, with most of the equipment in reasonable condition. Apart from the tree house 'nest' and a new fence, we intended to do very little in the bottom third of the garden.

We were able to follow the agreed brief quite closely, as most of the problems we faced were ones which had to be overcome first in order to meet the brief, rather than ones which stopped us being able to achieve our objectives. Our biggest problem was the weather conditions, which were appalling for garden construction.

We had to make several changes to the original design. One of these was at the top of the garden, close to the garage, where we had intended to break up and remove a section of the concrete patio and replace it with a planting-pit for ornamental plants.

Not only would this have looked attractive, but it would also have improved the surface drainage from the patio. The change of plan occurred when we discovered a drainage inspection cover and realized that beneath the point where we had intended to remove the concrete there was a drain connected to the sewerage system. This meant that we could not risk breaking up the concrete after all; the area remained patio though it was given a different surface.

We also had problems of space and access, particularly in terms of dismantling the existing garden and constructing the new one. There was very limited access into and out of the rear garden, and most of the materials to be discarded had to be wheelbarrowed out through the garage to a skip parked in the drive, with access, at its narrowest point, restricted to a single doorway. The new materials were delivered to a holding area covering the garden, drive and pathway at the front of the house, and everything then had to be carefully taken through the garage and out into the garden. To make matters worse, the side door to the garage opened out on to the patio area, which was having quite a lot of brickwork done around it, and again this limited access and movement. However, we tried to plan the carrying and positioning of materials to make life as

▲ *The Berkshire garden as we found it, prior to hard landscaping.*

easy as possible. When we actually started the construction, for example, we even carried all the compost and mulch through the garage and down to the bottom of the garden, in order to try and gain some working space.

Without a doubt, the most disappointing aspect of this garden was the very thing all gardeners talk about regardless of how good or bad it is – the weather. It rained almost non-stop from start to finish, and when the heavy rain eased, it drizzled, just for a change. We spent so much time simply trying to combat the weather that we gradually fell behind schedule, and to everyone's disappointment, we were unable to finish all we had set out to do in the allotted time. However, Trevor (Spider) Webb and students from Berkshire College of Agriculture worked an extra day to see the job through, and, of course, the sun shone all that day, when the rest of us had left.

Hard Landscaping

Much of the work took the form of reshaping and replanting an existing layout, rather than complete reconstruction. Having said that, the changes we made had quite a dramatic effect. We started by clearing the site of all the plants which Meri had decided to keep. She had a collection of herbaceous geraniums which were obvious candidates for keeping, and these, with various others which were to be kept, were lifted carefully and taken just outside the garden to the edge of the woodland, where they were 'heeled in' to be used later. Most of these plants would be re-introduced into the garden later; those which were not were distributed among Meri's gardening friends and neighbours.

The panel fence at the bottom of the garden was removed and discarded, together with the tree house and the legs which supported it. The existing patio was a sub-base which had been laid the previous year but not actually finished, so its front edge was trimmed to run parallel to the back of the house. The lawn was dug up and the turf was incorporated into the soil to help improve the fertility, which was very poor. Meri had done a marvellous job to grow any plants at all, as we did not find a single worm in this area of the garden (never a good sign).

The brickwork for the garden path and patio was started next. This would take the entire three days (and, because of the weather, would still not be finished). Setting out and marking the positions of all the key features (such as corners) became really tedious, and we spent ages wondering why the path did not look quite right. We finally discovered that it was because the wall of the house and the fence line, both of which had been used as 'base lines' on the plan, were actually not at right-angles to one another, and we had to make a few minor adjustments to achieve the required visual effect. The brick border was laid down the garden to form the outer limits of the path, followed by brick spars which ran across the path at 1m (3ft) intervals along its length. We then marked out and started work on the patio, creating a 'grid' of 1m (3ft) brick sections. Once the mortar had finally set, we filled most of the squares with gravel, level with the top edge of the bricks. This gravel was then firmed lightly with rakes, thoroughly drenched with water, and compacted again, this time using a motorized vibrating plate to give a firm surface. The hardness of this surface is the result of the many different particle sizes of gravel being washed and settled by the water and then bound together when the pressure of the vibrating plate is applied.

We dug three holes 1m (3ft) deep for the three posts which were to support the new tree house, and as ever, we experienced mixed fortunes. We had extreme difficulty in digging the holes without damaging any large tree roots, but this option was a far better one than nailing posts to the trunks of live trees and risking the prospect of encouraging them to start decaying. The good luck came in the form of a new type of quick-drying cement which we were using for the first time, a magical formula which set solid within half an hour of adding water to it. This meant that we could start to construct the platform on the top of the supports with hardly any delay. This was done by Dick, ably assisted by students from the Berkshire College of Agriculture.

The new tree house on top of this platform was constructed from hazel twigs, woven together to form a three-sided bird's nest. Into the fabric of the nest were woven brightly-coloured twigs of red, green and blue. Rings covered with brightly-coloured tapestry and cloth were wired on to the outside of the nest.

To divide the two sections of the garden, and to cope with its slope, we built a retaining wall to a height of 75cm (2½ft), with a step built into it, at the end of the garden path. This step, and the retaining wall, were built out of rustic logs to blend with the woodland setting.

Materials and equipment

Treated posts (4m/12ft)
Tannelized wood for treehouse 1.5m x 6in x 1in
Bricks, red matched (1,000)
Gravel – CED Cedec Gold (1cu m)
Turf, hard-wearing shade mix (40sq m)
Sharp sand (2cu m)
Quick-drying cement
Post and rail fence (1.2m/4ft)
Post and rail gate
Hinges and catch
Rabbit wire (1¼in/3cm)
Mix 'N' Mulch (50 x 80 litres)
Resin-coated slow-release fertilizer
Ornamental bark for mulch (50 bags)
2 Large Thai urns
Hazel pea-sticks (200 x 2m)
Rubbish skip
Wheelbarrows
Vibrating plate
Sledgehammer
Concrete mixer – small
Brick cutter
Scaffolding planks

Soft Landscaping

Because of Meri's love for the woodland it was obvious it should be a vital link with the garden. The planting would reflect this, becoming less wild and more ornamental, as it approached the house. The larchlap fences would be completely softened with foliage and the view would be opened up at the bottom of the garden so that there would be a feeling that the land extended beyond its boundaries. Once the garden had been reorganized, its focal point became the green turf and brick path which pointed

▲ The hazel and sambucus will begin to separate the lower part of the garden in two to three years. The bamboo and climbers soften the paving by the house.

▶ The garden after three months. The bamboo will grow up to cover the brick wall, and shrubs and climbers will soften the perimeter of the garden, blending it with the woodland beyond.

▼ The new tree house being woven from coppiced hazel twigs.

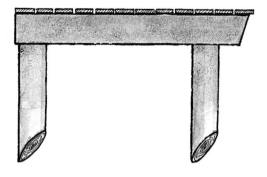

▲ **Tree-house platform (side view): this was constructed as a raised deck and was supported on a tripod of sturdy wooden posts, concreted into the ground.**

towards the distant trees. The lawn was positioned so that it was away from the drip-line of the trees and linked the terrace with the garden.

The beds in the top section of the garden formed a marked contrast with the informal planting at the edge of the woodland. Despite their strong outlines, their contents would be repeatedly informal, a mix of small trees, shrubs and ground cover. The key plants in the lower part of the garden were chosen to partially screen the play area below and yet allow views through and beyond. Two large clumps of copper hazel were positioned informally on each side of the garden to make a dark background, and the laciniated elder was planted in front of the neighbouring garage to help screen the walls. The use of lacy foliage as a screen provided a background without an obvious focus, thus softening and blurring the boundaries. The use of native plants or their varieties provided a link with the woodland beyond.

Closer to the house the key plants were chosen for their rich greenery – the majority evergreen, to soften the lines of the building and provide winter interest. The deciduous woodland already had a

winter structure which needed to be established closer to the house. Bamboo was repeated on each side of the garden, planted both as a rigid screen and more informally. *Choisya* 'Aztec Pearl', with its fine foliage, and the architectural *Fatsia japonica* were used to link the evergreens together, with *Hedera colchica* to continue the evergreen theme into the lower garden.

The terrace was partially screened from the garden by a planting of silvery coyote willow, which with its fine graceful growth would create a sense of enclosure without dominating and forming a solid screen. The willows would be an excellent foil for the plants in the border and would prevent a feeling that the garden was planted around the edges. Planting tall subjects at the front introduced a greater sense of depth and another distraction from the garden's perimeter. For the winter we interplanted the framework with the white-stemmed bramble *Rubus thibetanus* 'Silver Fern' to give an informal atmosphere and lightness in the shade.

The fences were softened with climbers, the large billowing *Clematis* 'Bill Mackenzie' behind the bamboo in the more ornamental area and a large-leaved *Vitis coignetiae* to clothe the house and add drama to the lush planting there. The green ivy running the entire length of the larchlap fence was softened with a selected wild form of honeysuckle, *Lonicera periclymenum* 'Graham Thomas'. Its cream flowers coupled with interplanted white clematis would give the dark ivy an essential lift.

Two urns were planted with white regale lilies for their luminosity in the shade and as a dramatic reminder that the woodland feel was after all in the context of a garden. The golden *Hakonechloa macra* 'Albovariegata' was planted with them to provide a splash of light when the lilies were out of bloom.

The next step was to interplant the shrubs with drifts of perennials designed to link all the areas together. Ground cover such as *Tellima grandiflora* and evergreen *Geranium macrorrhizum* 'Album' were introduced first, with deciduous perennials interplanted to rise up through the ground-protecting mat of foliage. We used foxgloves and ferns to mimic the woodland, with woodland plants and shade-tolerant species so that the planting would be almost entirely self-sufficient. No staking would be needed and the garden would have a relaxed atmosphere, each plant mingling with the next to produce a multi-layered effect in keeping with the woodland edge.

To capitalize on the cool nature of the garden and make the most of the relatively low light levels, many of the plants were chosen for their soft gentle growth and white flowers. In June white foxgloves would push through a ground cover of green-belled tellima into the white-flowered laciniated elder, while later in the season the white spikes of persicaria would be picked up by the tapers of cimicifuga. Blue flowers were also chosen for their ability to 'hover' in shade. We used dark *Aconitum* 'Spark's Variety' and low ferny *Corydalis cashmeriana*. The last introduction was a large clump of an ornamental grass, *Molinia altissima* 'Transparent', planted in one of the squares of the terrace to provide a gauzy screen.

When it came to planting, the rain actually worked to our advantage, as there was no need whatever to water the plants in. We actually did most of the planting standing on planks of wood, to prevent too much compaction of the soil and to stop things getting too muddy. As soon as we had finished planting one section of garden, we scattered a top-dressing of a resin-coated slow-release fertilizer over the beds and lightly pricked it into the soil with forks.

When we had finished all of the planting, we were

Plants and seeds

Acanthus latifolius
Aconitum 'Spark's Variety'
Ajuga reptans
Akebia quinata
Alchemilla mollis
Angelica archangelica
Choisya 'Aztec Pearl'
Cimicifuga racemosa 'Purpurea'
Clematis 'Bill Mackenzie'
Clematis 'Marie Boisselot'
Corydalis flexuosa 'Père David'
Corylus maxima 'Purpurea'
Dicentra spectabilis 'Alba'
Digitalis purpurea
Dryopteris felix-mas
Epimedium x perralchicum
Fatsia japonica
Galium odoratum
Geranium macrorrhizum 'Album'
Geranium phaeum
Hakonechloa macra 'Albovariegata'
Hedera colchica
Helleborus foetidus
Hydrangea aspera (H. villosa)
Hydrangea sargentiana
Iris foetidissima
Lilium regale
Lonicera periclymenum 'Graham Thomas'
Luzula maxima 'Marginata'
Molinia caerulea 'Variegata'
Nicotiana affinis 'White Cloud'
Phyllostachys aurea
Polygonum amplexicaule
Polygonum multiflorum
Pulmonaria saccharata 'Sissinghurst White'
Rubus thibetanus 'Silver Fern'
Salix exigua
Sambucus nigra 'Laciniata'
Sarcococca hookeriana var. digyna
Tellima grandiflora
Tropaeolum speciosum
Vitus coignetiae

quite lavish with our use of organic material for mulching. As well as being the usual method of suppressing weeds, we were particularly keen on bringing about an improvement in the soil to help the plants establish. We wanted to cover the soil and reduce evaporation of moisture to an absolute minimum, but, most importantly, we also knew that we needed to encourage the rapid colonization of the soil by worms and bacteria – the only effective way to improve soil fertility on a lasting basis.

▲ **Dryopteris felix-mas** *and* **Geranium macrorrhizum 'Album'**.

▼ **Tellima grandiflora** *provides year-round evergreen ground cover, protecting the soil from draught and heavy drips from the trees above. Its green flowers in April provide a soft vertical accent amongst shrubs.*

▶ **Lilium regale** *in the large urn. Sweet woodruff and* **Pulmonaria saccharata 'Sissinghurst White'** *at the base as ground cover. Staggered features such as the urn provide a narrative as you pass through the garden to the gate and into the woodland.*

Nottinghamshire

A Village Community Garden
Nottinghamshire

The Client

The site for this community garden is a former mining village on the Nottinghamshire/Derbyshire border, part of an area which has been through some pretty hard times in recent years, with pit closures, declining industry, high unemployment and the general lack of resources associated with these circumstances. To some extent the village has appeared to turn in on itself, with the population of this tightly-knit community helping each other through the bad times.

The concept of this garden came mainly from the energy and determination of three quite extraordinary women, Kath, Elaine and Hazel, who decided that the time had come for the village to start to revitalize itself. In order to start things off, they need to have a focus, something for everyone – a safe place for children to play, a peaceful spot for senior citizens to sit, and an area where anybody could sit for a minute or two and watch the world go by. They had already made a start on the piece of land which they wanted to develop. The children were to be included in the project, and they wanted the garden to be respected by the community as a special space – and a welcoming feature to those entering the village.

The land was divided into two: a grassed area and the section which had been cleared by the community the previous autumn. They wanted

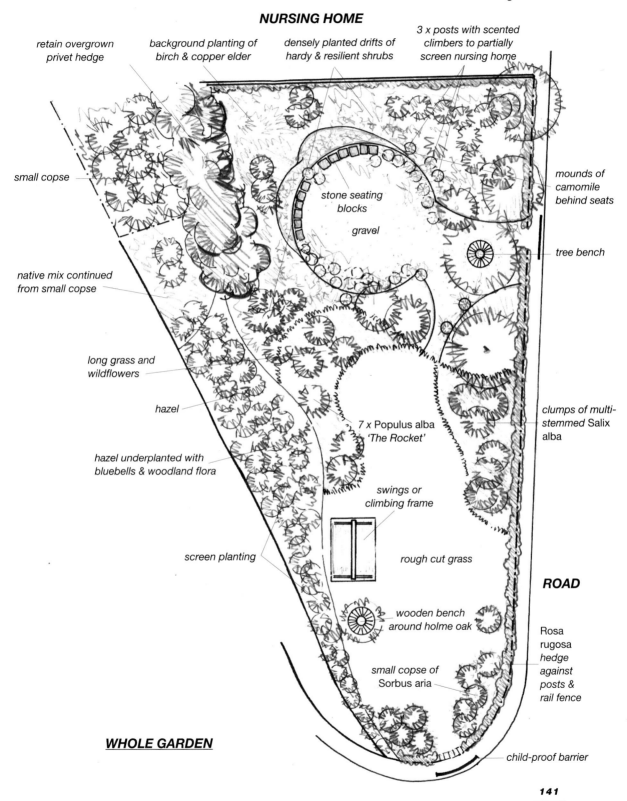

NURSING HOME

retain overgrown
privet hedge

background planting of
birch & copper elder

densely planted drifts of
hardy & resilient shrubs

3 x posts with scented
climbers to partially
screen nursing home

small copse

stone seating
blocks

gravel

mounds of
camomile
behind seats

tree bench

native mix continued
from small copse

long grass and
wildflowers

hazel

7 x Populus alba
'The Rocket'

clumps of multi-
stemmed Salix
alba

hazel underplanted with
bluebells & woodland flora

swings or
climbing frame

screen planting

rough cut grass

ROAD

wooden bench
around holme oak

Rosa
rugosa
hedge
against
posts &
rail fence

WHOLE GARDEN

small copse of
Sorbus aria

child-proof barrier

▲ *A former mining village on the Nottinghamshire/*
Derbyshire border: the site for the community garden.
▼ *Kath, Elaine and Hazel on the camomile bench.*

to develop the cleared section as a flower garden and have a seating area with benches around the trees. The grassed area would be a knock-around area for the children. It was vital that the land be securely fenced off from the road, and that the paths should be able to accommodate wheelchairs from the nearby nursing home.

They were not specific about plants, but envisaged shrubs and flowers that would still be interesting in the cold winter months.

The Diagnosis

The area of land to be used for the garden was all but derelict, and we first saw it after Kath, Elaine and Hazel had organized a clean-up with the willing help of children from the local school and youth club. The site still had bricks, rubble, tarmac, concrete foundations, wire, tin cans and a fine collection of perennial weeds.

It was roughly triangular, with a cart track on one boundary, a busy main road into the village on the second, and a wooden fence beside a senior citizens' residential home on the third. There were several mature trees, including sycamore and horse chestnut, close to the road, and a substantial privet hedge on the opposite boundary by the cart track. Approximately two-thirds of the site was rough grass,

punctuated with brambles and dock, but these had been cut down to stumps when the site was tidied up. There had also been a number of bonfires in this section, leaving us with the disposal of car tyre remains, partly burned-through logs, and a lot of charred tin cans and bottles.

The site was open, with no existing fences at all on the road side, and this presented a very real problem – there had been two children fatally injured in traffic accidents on this road during recent years. The site naturally divided into two quite distinct areas: a community garden at the lowest and broadest end of the site (close to the senior citizens' residence), which could be quite formal in layout, and the bulk of the site as grassland, planted with clumps of native trees and a safe play area for children. In one respect we arrived just in time, because this grassland area was due to be sprayed with weedkiller and we were able to advise against this course of action. As things turned out, this advice actually led to the development of an established grass play area with a reasonable surface, much quicker than had been anticipated.

Perhaps the single most frustrating issue on this site was that we were unable to finish everything we had set out to do, which meant that we did not see the final results. When we left, the fence had not been finished (the slow rate at which the concrete set

slowed us down), and we had not been able to start planting the rose hedge for that reason.

What really slowed down the entire operation was the discovery of a wall foundation running parallel to the pathway along the roadside. This brick and concrete base was at least 23cm (9in) wide and 60cm (2ft) deep, and to make matters worse, it ran along the very line on which we intended to build a fence and plant a hedge. We also had a few anxious moments when two pipes running across the middle of the site were uncovered, but these were carefully checked and it transpired that they had been redundant for a good many years. This was a great relief to us all, as the pipes were just where our most important access path would be excavated.

The established trees which we decided to retain on the site also presented a problem, as we were reluctant to prune or severely damage any of their roots. This meant that where the old crumbling paths ran close to the trees, we had to break up and remove all the tarmac and rubble by hand rather than use machinery. This was not a task any of us enjoyed, particularly as this area had once been used as a site for dumping soot, some of which drifted up to give us all a light dusting. The shallow depth of some of the tree roots also forced us to raise the height of one section of path rather than damage them.

◄ *The site of the community garden in Nottinghamshire (showing the section designated for the main seating area) after the initial clearance of Day 1. The size and scale of this site meant that an excavator had to be used to clear existing walls and paths. Then the soil was moved until the levels were correct and the hard landscaping could be started.*

Hard Landscaping

Because of the size and scale of the site, and bearing in mind the amount of earth and rubble to be moved, we used an excavator to work on the breaking up of walls and paths. Once everything on the site was cleared and stacked in the appropriate areas, we could get some indication of what we had to work with and a rough idea of what our finished levels were likely to be.

The initial earthworks had been started when we returned to begin the garden proper, and the change was quite noticeable. The double brick wall in the centre of the site was a gaping hole in the ground, and all the rubble, bricks and concrete pieces were arranged, just as we had requested, in a low mound running roughly parallel to the privet hedge, with all the material spread out and compacted. We started by measuring out and marking the position of the central circular area, and once this was fixed, we marked out the pathways leading to it.

Materials and equipment
Excavator
Treated posts (64m)
Post Fix (8 large bags)
Lawn edging (80m)
Gravel – Cedec Red (3cu m)
Scalpings (3cu m)
Sharp sand (1cu m)
Cement (10 bags)
Builder's sand (1cu m)
Woodland chipped bark (60 x 80 litres)
Pig wire for length of fence (30m/98ft)
Mulch 'N' Mix (40 x 80 litres)
Vibrating plate
Wheelbarrows
3-Bar post and rail fence
Stone and wood seating
Rotary mower

PLANTING PLAN & ORNAMENTAL AREA

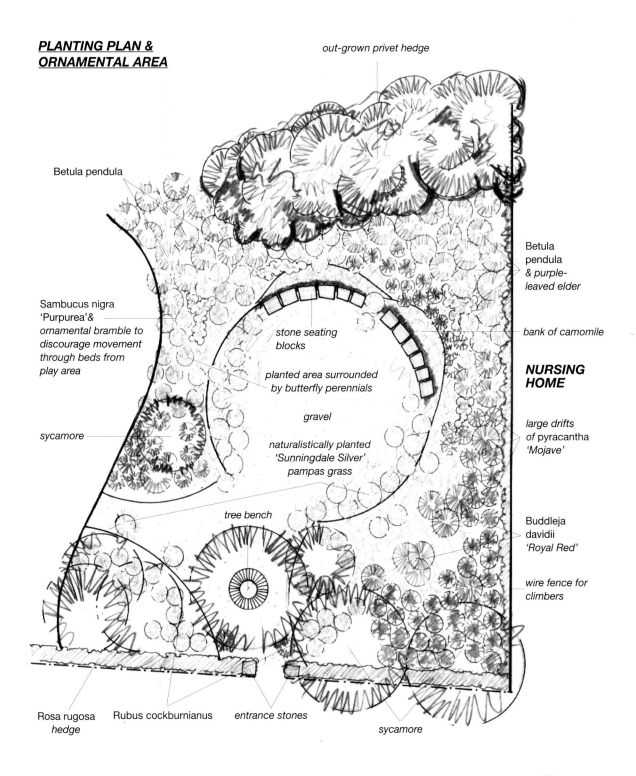

out-grown privet hedge

Betula pendula

Betula pendula & purple-leaved elder

bank of camomile

Sambucus nigra 'Purpurea' & ornamental bramble to discourage movement through beds from play area

stone seating blocks

planted area surrounded by butterfly perennials

NURSING HOME

gravel

large drifts of pyracantha 'Mojave'

sycamore

naturalistically planted 'Sunningdale Silver' pampas grass

tree bench

Buddleja davidii 'Royal Red'

wire fence for climbers

Rosa rugosa hedge

Rubus cockburnianus

entrance stones

sycamore

▲ *The three-bar fence and* Rosa rugosa *hedge designed to protect the garden from the road.*
▶ *Three months on, a view into the garden from the top lawn.*
▼ *Local children help plant the gravel circle with pampass grass and* Eschscholzia.

▲ *Eventually, shrubs will enclose the retreat and shelter it from the road. The birch in the foreground will screen out the nursing home and provide a soft lacy background to the main planting.*

The excavator scraped and moved soil for us until the levels were right and the paths had all been cut out to the correct size and level, and we then moved over this area compacting it with a motorized vibrating plate. The ground was so hard here that we were able to place gravel directly on to the compacted soil sub-base.

The central area needed to be suitable for mothers pushing prams and buggies, people in wheelchairs, and senior citizens who might not be too steady on their feet, so we had to make a firm all-weather surface. The main hard landscaping here consisted of laying about 20 tonnes of 'pink gravel' and compacting it with a motorized vibrating plate. Once we had the levels about right, the gravel was thoroughly drenched with water and compacted again, to give a firm surface. To keep this in place, we marked out the area with plastic lawn edging, to prevent the soil and gravel mixing together. Opposite the main entrance to the site, two stone bench-type seats were made using old reclaimed stone from a nearby railway bridge which had been demolished. These very large stone sections were manhandled and cemented into position by our site foreman, Trevor (Spider) Webb, with the help of landscaping students from the local agricultural college based at Easton in Derbyshire.

The post and rail fence was erected by members of a charitable organization, part of the local groundwork trust, who had to put up with appalling conditions for erecting a fence. We wondered why it was taking them so long to erect each post, and soon discovered the reason for the slow progress – the hidden wall foundation that ran parallel to the pathway along the roadside. We spoke nicely to Aiden, our friendly and very helpful excavator driver, and even though his machine struggled to take out a couple of the post holes in the foundations, he was able to do the job for us in a very short period of time.

Soft Landscaping

This community garden was divided into two distinct areas: the top lawn with its play area and rough grass, and the garden proper with seating and planting. Harsh weather conditions, poor soil and the need to plant tough, long-lived and vandal-resistant plants made the plant list very specific, and apart from a handful of perennials, the plants were selected for their ready availability and endurance.

The first task was to fence the site off to prevent children straying on to the road. A double row of *Rosa rugosa* was to be planted along the fence, to welcome visitors to the village as they drove in.

The top lawn, which was to become the memorial garden (to the children who had been victims of road accidents) and play area, was planted entirely with pale- and silver-foliaged trees to lighten the atmosphere. We planted a group of *Sorbus aria* 'Lutescens' on either side of the entrance, and a small copse of the fastigiate white poplar on the top side as a focal point. These were linked to a dense group of silver willow, *Salix alba* 'Sericea', which would form bushy trees on the roadside. A solitary native oak was planted as the memorial tree. The trees chosen needed to be strong growers, as the grass under the trees would be left long to blend in with the landscaped slagheaps behind. A small spinney of hazel, wild rose and hawthorn was planted along the track to enclose the area and blend with the planting of young native species which had already been started by the Council. The feel of the top lawn would be rough and informal.

The willows were continued down into the main garden, which was designed to feel like a more private enclosure. After the re-landscaping of the soil, we planted an arc of the native silver birch, using young trees so that they would need the minimum of staking. The arc of birch was planted close, to shade out competition and provide a delicate backdrop to the garden which would blend in with the landscape beyond. Underneath, on bare earth, we sowed a woodland wildflower mix containing species such as foxglove and campion for spring interest. To continue the feel of the wild but to introduce a slightly more garden feel, the purple-leaved elder was planted in recesses left among the birch – its dark leaves would be a good foil to the garden and a contrast to the lightness of the birch. The planting partially obscured the nursing home behind, and three tall posts were erected and planted with vigorous rambling roses and honeysuckle to complete the screening of the building.

From this point, the planting became more ornamental. The entire length of the fence was planted with vigorous rambling clematis and *Vitis coignetiae* which would be allowed to scramble over the inner shrubs and obscure the ugly boundary under soft growth. The clematis can be cut back to the fence with shears as and when it becomes too overgrown.

The inner planting was composed of sweeping groups of pyracantha which would be encouraged to grow into loose shrubs. They would help to prevent vandalism problems with their thorny growth and would add a solid bulk to the scheme, an evergreen element, with rich winter berries and spring flowers to make a link to the elder. The orange-peel clematis behind would mingle with them.

The pyracantha was broken up by two clumps of a large-growing buddleja and several clumps of the giant herbaceous *Eupatorium maculatum*

Plants and seeds

Betula pendula
Buddleja davidii 'Royal Red'
Chamaemelum nobile 'Treneague'
Clematis 'Bill Mackenzie'
Cortaderia selloana 'Sunningdale Silver'
Corylus avellana
Crataegus monogyna
Echinacea purpurea
Eupatorium maculatum 'Atropurpureum'
Fagus sylvatica
Fraxinus excelsior
Lonicera periclymenum 'Serotina'
Nepeta 'Six Hills Giant'
Populus alba 'The Rocket'
Pyracantha 'Mojave'
Pyracantha x 'Watereri'
Quercus robur
Rosa glauca
Rosa rugosa
Rosa 'Wedding Day'
Rubus cockburnianus
Salix alba 'Sericea'
Sambucus nigra 'Purpurea'
Sedum spectabile 'Autumn Joy'
Sorbus aria 'Lutescens'
Symphytum 'Hidcote Pink'
Vinca major
Vitis coignetiae

SEEDS
Helianthus 'Velvet Queen'
Helianthus 'Russian Giant'
Nasturtium 'Trailing Mixed'
Wildflower Shade Mix to cover 100m²

▲ *(Left) Young pampass, catmint and* Sedum.

▲ *(Right) Flowers of* Sambucus nigra *'Purpurea' about to open.*

▶ *The camomile bench with a background of catmint and* Sedum *'Autumn Joy'.*

◀ *(Top) Immediately after planting. Young birch and copper elder to screen the garden from the top lawn.*

◀ *(Bottom) The same view three months later.*

'Atropurpureum' to rise up and through it and give seasonal fluctuation. The eupatorium would provide drama and winter forms to contrast with the birch and pyracantha. At the entrance to the garden large groupings of the white-stemmed *Rubus cockburnianus* were added, to prevent children taking a short cut through the beds.

Once the shrubs and trees were positioned, we introduced ground-cover plants to carpet the soil under herbaceous shrubs, add winter interest and suppress weed growth. The ground cover was chosen for its shade-tolerance and endurance in harsh conditions; low-carpeting comfrey was interplanted with periwinkle and encouraged to drift and mingle to give the planting a more naturalistic quality.

The soil mounds behind the stone seats were planted with camomile, a scented backrest. The plants will soon spread to cover the entire bank. The inner section of the planting, around the circular gravel area, was drifted with a mix of perennials to attract butterflies and to soften the edges. The ground planting was a mix of catmint and sedum, with interplanted echinacea pushing through to tie in with the giant eupatoriums behind.

The gravel was randomly scattered with a massed planting of pampas grass, placed to simulate wild drifts in a giant sweep and give a sense of excitement when entering the park. The gravel was sown with eschscholzia which would flower quickly and self-seed, and the children planted sunflowers in all the gaps between the shrubs for a dramatic show in year one.

On our first visit to the site we had advised against the use of weedkiller, pointing out that killing the grass, and then cultivating this site, would create far greater problems than those already existing. As it stood, the grass was actually suppressing the germination of weed seeds, but if the grass had been killed off and the ground cultivated, then millions of weed seeds would be exposed to daylight, the very element that most of them need to promote germination. We suggested a regime of frequent mowing, gradually lowering the height of the cutting blade, to thicken up the grass, and gradually kill out most of the weeds. This actually created an established play area much quicker than had been anticipated.

When we started the soft landscaping and planting, the first thing we did was to walk carefully over the rough grass area looking for any debris that might damage the mower. As soon as we had cleared the site, we cut the grass twice with a rotary mower, the first cut at about 10cm (4in), followed immediately by a second cut set at about 6cm (2½in), to start killing the unwanted weed species. We hope this section of lawn area will be mown closely at 10cm (4in) for the next three years to kill off the weeds. After this time, the grass will be left to grow naturally and allow native species to colonize and establish. Once the grass has reached this stage, the only regular mowing needed will be to demarcate walkways so that natural pathways are created through this naturalized area.

We did not have time to plant the hedge, but on the last day before we left we gave Kath, Hazel and Elaine a demonstration of how the job should be done, so that they could continue the planting with members of the local youth club. When it is in place, this *Rosa rugosa* hedge will be used to define the boundary of the garden alongside the busy main road. This plant is ideal as a hedge, being notoriously thorny, flowering prolifically, producing copious quantities of hips and requiring very little pruning.

As we finished planting each area, we mulched the plants to a 10cm (4in) depth with organic matter, followed by a thorough watering. Much of the watering was done by our 'little helpers' from the local school, and at times it appeared that the plants only received the water after the children had missed their aim when squirting each other with our hosepipe.

Hard Landscaping

3

The term 'hard landscaping' covers the construction of elements within a design, such as the paths and paved areas, which will provide the structure, or bones, of your garden. This is the framework which will later be filled in with the trees, shrubs and other plants – often referred to as the 'soft landscaping' of the garden. It will also provide the link which will tie the elements of the garden together, and should 'flow', or blend, rather than appear bitty and haphazard.

There are a wide variety of surfaces, structures and materials which can be used in the garden as alternatives, or complements, to the lawn. These can form paths and seating areas, create play structures, provide plant support and enclose water features.

Within the eleven gardens featured in the series, many hard-landscaping features were used, some more than once, and others in similar ways though for different purposes.

Site clearance

It is understandable, when faced with taking on a new garden or revamping an older one, to want to impose your own style and personality upon the garden as soon as possible. However, if the garden is an older one, do try to be patient if you can, particularly if you have taken over during the winter. Many of the plants you have inherited will be dormant, and until you know what you have to work with, it is

▶ *Wood is an ideal material to give a warm, natural feel in the garden and so is frequently used for hard landscaping.*

advisable not to rush into a programme of complete clearance. If you wait until one growing season has passed, it will give you the chance to identify the plants, assess what condition they are in, and see how they perform. You can then decide which plants to keep and which ones to get rid of.

The plants you decide to keep will not only save on costs, especially if they are larger specimens, but they will give an immediate look of maturity to the new garden.

Most plants can be moved, with care, to more appropriate places, provided that they are not too large and that the timing is right. If your plans include major changes to the garden, it may be worth considering moving any plants you want to keep to a temporary growing area until the garden is ready for them. This reduces the chances of plants being damaged by accident, and makes working on the site much easier.

Where existing hard-landscape features, such as ponds or paving, are concerned, you need to consider whether or not they have a part to play in the new garden. Check with the relevant organizations to determine whether or not there are any services (gas, water, electricity, telephone, cable TV) running through the site before deciding which structural features to remove or embarking on any excavations.

Rubbish removal

A site cleared of any movable obstructions or clutter will be a better and safer place to work, and whenever possible, it is desirable to clear the areas of all rubbish before work begins. However, it is essential to take great care when removing unwanted materials, in terms both of safety and of possible re-use on site. For example, surplus material arising

from clearing unwanted constructions and paving should be examined to see whether or not it can be recycled, if only as hardcore. Why pay to have the old material removed, then pay again to have something very similar delivered?

Don't be fooled by a new garden which appears clear – the ground may still contain vast quantities of builders' rubbish (we encountered this problem in the communal garden in Camberwell). Unfortunately, this is all too common where developers have been at work, and where a token few inches of topsoil is used to camouflage all manner of waste, which will need to be removed.

Local authorities tend to have very strict rules on the collection and dumping of rubbish, and of garden refuse in particular. Often the amount of rubbish will justify the use of a skip, and if this is the case, always check with the local police station in case there are guidelines for the placement and safety of skips, especially when parked on a public highway. In busy or built-up areas, some form of licence or permit may have to be applied for if a skip is required; if you have any doubts, always check.

Setting out

The next stage after clearing the site is 'setting out' or 'marking out'. This refers to marking the positions and dimensions of all the key elements in plan form on the ground, including walls (and the size and depth of any foundations), paths, sitting areas, lawn, pools, and even the position of certain individual plants. It is a task which involves the transfer of the information from the plan down on to the ground, and accuracy is crucial if the garden is to be an exact replica of the design.

The use of pegs and lines has long been the traditional way of marking out, and although it can be rather fiddly and time-consuming, it does have the advantage of being adjustable and giving a strong visual indication. Tall pegs or canes can be used to indicate the positions of individual specimen trees. When the marking out has been completed, it should be possible to walk through the proposed garden and, with the help of a little imagination, predict its final appearance. This is always a good way of getting some 'spatial awareness', and is an ideal time to make minor adjustments if they are felt to be necessary.

With straight lines, wooden pegs can be driven into the ground and string lines (use a brightly-coloured string so it is easy to see). Where a wall or an area of paving is planned, the pegs will represent the corners of the structure and the string line the outer edges. This gives you a good idea of the shape and size of the new structure but it is also an indication of the surface area which is to be worked on.

Curved lines obviously cannot be represented by making the builder's line straight, and in this instance, pegs or canes are spaced at appropriate distances to mark out the curve or circle. A string line is then laid in front or behind the canes, and pulled as tightly as possible to represent the curve. The closer together the pegs are, the more accurate the line of the true curve will be.

It may be easier when marking out curves to use a garden hose. Placing the hosepipe on the ground and moving it about to conform to the canes or pegs can give a reasonable degree of accuracy. Dry sand can then be trickled alongside the hose, and when the hose is removed a curve or circle is left on the ground.

Finally, where a shape or structure is being marked out on a hard surface, chalk can be used for measuring and marking out. This is usually followed up by knocking in metal spikes or pegs to make the markings more permanent, because the chalk markings are only temporary, and the first shower of rain will wash away all your hard work.

When the marking out is complete, always make a final check, as it's much easier for adjustments to be made now rather than later when the garden is under construction. Care taken during the initial surveying and planning operations will pay dividends later.

Setting levels

The original survey and diagnosis of the garden should show the angle of any slope (the amount of rise or fall) in the ground. The most efficient means of establishing levels is by using optical instruments: a 'dumpy level' for example, or just a spirit level and a plank of wood with a straight edge to it.

It is a good idea to make cross-sectional drawings, depending on the nature of the level changes. To achieve the full benefit from cross-sectional drawings, they should preferably be drawn to a scale to match that of the main survey drawing.

SITE LEVELLING

Add or remove soil from between the pegs until the soil surface is an equal distance from the line marked on each peg.

Wooden pegs knocked into the ground with a marker pen.

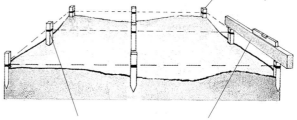

Make a line 10cm from the top of the peg.

Use a straight-edged board and spirit level to set the correct levels.

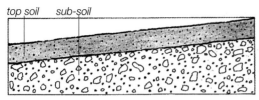

top soil   sub-soil

TOP SOIL REMOVED

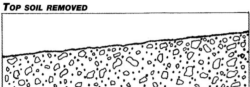

SUB SOIL LEVELLED

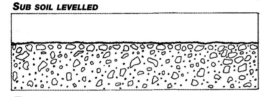

TOP SOIL REPLACED

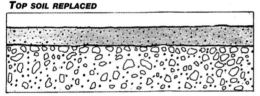

▲ *The 'cut and fill' technique used to level a sloping site, as in the Cornwall garden.*

The chosen line on which the changes in level are indicated will also need a horizontal companion-line to show the difference in levels. These cross-sectional drawings will show existing levels, which can then be compared with the proposed changes.

The implications of how much material may need to be excavated and removed or, alternatively, imported or moved to make up levels, can then be calculated. These calculations are necessary to determine such things as numbers of steps, and grass slopes. When dealing with levels against a house wall, the finished level must be 15cm (6in) below the damp-proof course (two courses of bricks). This is a particularly important consideration when dealing with patios and decks.

Bricks

Paving

Bricks are one of the oldest forms of paving material – they were widely used in the past wherever a usable clay was available, and they are still very popular today. The varied sources of clay and wide variety of patterns give brick paving a very special character. They can be hard-wearing, good to look at, and available in a wide range of colours, sizes and finishes. However, when laid on the ground, it must be remembered that bricks will be subjected to individual pressure of traffic and pedestrians, not the shared and evenly distributed pressure they are subjected to when built into a wall. Bricks tend to be used within a design to provide a link from one area in the garden to another, to create an effect within an enclosed space, or to form the space itself. A huge variety of patterns can be used, and each will have a slightly different effect on its environment.

In Robin's garden in Balham, the paving was planned to serve two purposes: first to act as a pathway, laid in a running bond pattern to make the narrow garden look wider, and second, in the sitting area, laid in a basketweave pattern, a square arrangement which has the effect of restricting the sense of movement and creating a feeling of stability. Bricks were also used to create terraces at each end of the communal garden in Camberwell, tying the design together by the repetitive use of the same surface.

The materials used were the same in both gardens: reclaimed bricks (London stocks). This is a yellow brick, with a warm appearance and a good texture.

Although laying brick paving may seem rather complicated, it can be a very rewarding project provided a few simple rules are followed:

- Always thoroughly compact the base of the area to be paved.
- Place a 2.5cm (1in) layer of dry loose sand over the area to 'bed' the bricks on to (if wet sand is used it takes on a fluid property, making it impossible to stabilize the paving).
- Fix the bricks into position by brushing fine, dry sand between them.

Design

When using brick paths in a design, it is important to bear the whole plan in mind, rather than just viewing the bricks in isolation. The way other individual units meet the paving patterns, and the junctions with other materials, should be carefully considered. You have to take the size of the bricks into consideration, and decide whether they are in keeping with the scale of the plan. The proposed pattern may, in fact, involve special units or an unacceptable amount of cutting.

A directional pattern may be required to emphasize a particular route, to provide better joint grip, or improve water run-off. This is particularly important when a certain effect is required, for example; turning bricks longways across a narrow area can give the illusion of width (Balham), or to get the eye to follow a particular line (Berkshire).

An interlocking pattern, such as herringbone, will prevent lateral movement of the bricks caused by heavy wear.

▲ *(Top)* **To leave a smooth recessed gap in brick joints, a small piece of hosepiping can be used.**

▲ **Meri and Dick's shade garden in Berkshire featured a patio and garden path consisting of a grid of brick sections which was filled with gravel and levelled across the top.**

159

brick pavers

retaining kerb

dry sand bed

compacted
sub-base

By taking advantage of the many differences in appearance, size, shape and colour of the bricks available, you can have a whole range of patterns to create interest within the garden.

Characteristics

Some of the building bricks used in wall construction, traditionally 210mm x 105mm x 65mm (8½ x 4in x 2¾in), can be used in the garden, but only bricks such as engineering bricks and hard burnt stocks are suitable for outdoor paving. This type of brick is graded as Category 'F' (defined as being resistant to frost damage even when water-saturated and subjected to repeated cycles of freezing and thawing). The suitability of any particular brick can be checked with the manufacturer or supplier, most of whom are now increasing the range of bricks available for use as external pavers.

A great deal of attention has been given to the appearance and texture of the upper face of the brick, the finish or texture of which will depend on the method of manufacture.

HAND-MADE, PRESSED OR WIRE-CUT

Hand-made bricks suitable for paving tend to vary considerably in terms of shape, size and density. They are expensive, and are only really justified on projects where a high-quality finish is required.

Pressed and **wire-cut** bricks are generally of a more consistent texture, and are more uniform. Some compressed brick pavers are closely related to engineering bricks and are made to similar specifications, but are less dense. They are smooth-surfaced, and for external use a stamped pattern is often added to prevent slipping and improve traction. Wire-cut or drag-faced pavers have a roughened surface which helps to make them less slippery.

▲ **Brush in dry sand to stabilize the brick pavers.**
This will reduce lateral movement.

Variations in the colour and texture of paving bricks are due to factors such as differing clay types and kiln-firing conditions. Depending on your point of view, these can be viewed as advantageous variations, as they will lend 'character' to an otherwise uniform area. However, a variation can also occur between batches, and for large projects. selection and mixing may be necessary at the factory in order to distribute the different pavers reasonably evenly, and give the impression that the mixture was deliberate and part of a blending process.

Construction

The traditional method of bedding pavers on coarse sand, known as 'flexible' construction, involves laying them with close-butt joints (2–5mm wide), filled with sand. A gap of this width is necessary to ensure that the sand can enter and develop a bond with the bricks by means of friction. Flexible paving, by its very nature, can 'creep', and must be supported around its perimeter by an edge-restraint of some kind, such as a brick trim, brick edge, concrete kerb, or channels, or be haunched in concrete.

Steps in constructing a paved area

1 Mark out an outline of the area, using pegs and string or a hosepipe. The pegs can also be used to indicate the desired levels.

2 Excavate (if necessary) the site to the required depth, which is a minimum of 5cm (2in), plus the depth of the chosen paving material, and compact the ground by hand or using a vibrating plate.

3 Add a layer of sand over the base and compact it by hand or by using a vibrating plate, then rake the surface lightly (to bed the bricks on to).

4 Start laying the bricks in rows (to the chosen pattern), press them in position and pack them fairly tightly together. Lay all the whole bricks first and insert the cut bricks as you finish.

5 Compact the paving, using a vibrating plate with a rubber sole (or use a layer of old carpet) to avoid damage to the bricks.

6 Cover the surface of the brick path or patio with dry sand and brush it into the joints.

7 Compact the area again, to settle the bricks and bed them in.

This work should only be carried out in dry weather to avoid weak construction. Flexible brick paving is not self-draining, and must be laid to proper falls.

Drainage falls

Adequate gradients are essential to drain the flexible brick paving, and the direction of the fall should follow the main joint lines. Gradients for both rigid and flexible brick paving should not be less than 1:60.

With paving, bricks can be laid either on their face, giving a ratio of length to width of 2:1, or on their edge, giving a ratio of 3:1. If the bricks are laid on their edge, 50 per cent more bricks will be required, and bricks less than 65mm thick are not suitable for laying in this way.

Common brick paving patterns

(A) STRETCHER (RUNNING) BOND

This can either run with the direction of traffic, or be set at right-angles across it. When setting it out to run with the direction of traffic, it is essential to have accurate edge restraints in order to prevent the lines of pavers from wavering. Quarter, half and third lap-bond can be used to accentuate the pattern. When laid as flexible paving, stretcher bond is sufficiently effective in locking the brick courses for pedestrian use, but is not strong enough for vehicles.

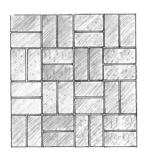

(B) BASKETWEAVE

This gives a number of pattern variations, based on a proportion of a 3:1 or 2:1 ratio. Larger areas can be subdivided into bays or strips by using bands of contrasting bricks, within which the pattern of basketweave paving is laid. As there are long, unbonded joints, it is not suitable for areas of flexible construction. If hand-made bricks are used they may need to be sorted to achieve a degree of uniformity.

(C) FLEMISH BOND

This is a very attractive but slightly more labour-intensive pattern, due to the amount of cutting needed. Flemish bond is regarded as a static pattern, is a good choice for areas where no sense of movement is required, and is often used as an alternative to basketweave.

A flemish bond pattern is achieved by laying four overlapping bricks to form a square and placing a half brick in the centre.

(D) HERRINGBONE

This is the best paver interlock for flexible paving and creates a regular pattern which can be viewed from any direction without changing the effect.

Herringbone is normally laid at 45 degrees to the edge of the paving, which will give the most visual tolerance if misalignment occurs, but can also be laid at 90 degrees to the edge. Herringbone looks its best when framed with a soldier course or, alternatively, a specially designed edging-block. The use of triangular specials will avoid the expense of cutting a lot of small edge pieces.

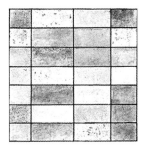

(E) STACK (GRID PATTERN) BOND

This decorative bond can be very effective in confined areas such as courtyards or small enclosed gardens, where it can echo the shape or form of a building. It has poor interlocking qualities, because of the continuous lines in both directions, and is used only for rigid, rather than flexible, construction.

(F) CIRCULAR OR CURVED PATTERNS

These can easily be created with bricks, due to their small unit size. You also have the flexibility of turning them on edge or on end, and using half-bricks. Smaller circles have to have a rigid construction, and circular patterns require a high degree of skill to obtain joints which are neither too wide nor too narrow, but it is worth the effort.

Walls

Walls are seldom simply decorative features – they usually perform at least one other function, such as providing security, boundary definition, shelter or screening, or a combination of these. Within the garden they can be used to screen off one area from another, retain soil on a split-level site, or divide the garden into sections.

Foundations

The purpose of a foundation is to transfer the weight of the wall to the ground below in a way which will enable it to remain stable throughout the year, despite changing weather conditions.

There are three aspects to this:

- The *foundation width* must be sufficient to spread the load over an adequate area of subsoil.
- The *foundation strength* must be sufficient to carry those stresses from the structure through to the subsoil.
- The *foundation depth* must be sufficient to ensure that it is not disturbed by the actions of frost or moisture movement.

For most garden walls a strip foundation is normally used.

Foundation dimensions for a wall (concrete strip foundation)

Type	Wall Height	Foundation Depth	Width
Single brick	1m	15cm	30cm
Double brick	1m	30cm	45cm
Double brick	1–2m	45cm	60cm
Retaining wall	1m	15–30cm	40cm

Strip foundation for a wall

1 Start by marking out the site of the foundation with string lines stretched taut between wooden pegs.

2 Dig a trench to the required depth, and make sure that the sides of the trench are vertical and the base is level.

3 Knock wooden pegs into the bottom of the trench so that their tops are at a point to match the final level of upper surface of the concrete.

4 Fill the bottom half of the trench with hardcore and compact it.

5 Pour in a concrete mix, chopping down into the wet mix with a shovel to settle the concrete and help to remove any bubbles.

6 Firm the concrete by patting it down to the required level with a piece of timber, but leave the final surface rough so that the brick mortar can key into it.

STRIP FOUNDATION (FOR A WALL)

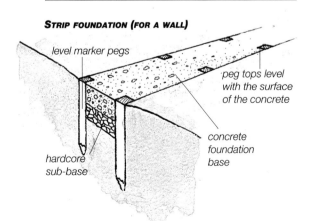

level marker pegs

peg tops level with the surface of the concrete

hardcore sub-base

concrete foundation base

Bricklaying

The first course: Mix up the mortar and tip it on to a mortar board close to the place where you are working.

Set up a string guideline to which you can lay the first course of bricks.

Using a builder's trowel, spread a 10mm (⅜in) thick layer of mortar centrally along the top of the concrete foundation, and drag the tip of your trowel through the mortar to create a furrow.

Place the first brick on the layer of mortar and align it with the string line, and flush with the proposed end of the wall.

Firmly press the brick into position by wiggling it to bed it firmly into the mortar. This will increase the bond between the brick, mortar and concrete foundation.

Applying this pressure often squeezes some mortar out from under the brick, so use the trowel to scoop this up and use it to form the vertical joint between first brick and the next one you lay.

Put some mortar onto the end of the second brick using the point of the trowel, forming a wedge-shape.

Place the second brick on the layer of mortar, and align it with the string line, with the mortared end flush against the end of the first brick.

Scoop up any excess mortar and use this as part of the process for laying the next brick in line. This procedure is repeated until the first course of bricks has been laid.

Lay a spirit level along the bricks to make sure the bricks are level; any which are too high can be tapped down into position using the base of the trowel handle.

The second course: In order for a strong bond to form, the bricks must overlap so that the joints of

LAYING A COURSE OF BRICKS

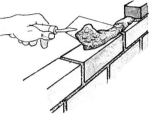

◀ **Trowel mortar on to the bricks of the previous course.**

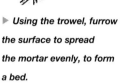

▶ **Using the trowel, furrow the surface to spread the mortar evenly, to form a bed.**

◀ **Butter the end of the next brick with mortar and mould the mortar into a wedge shape.**

▶ **Position the brick on top of the mortar bed. Butt the mortared end up against the adjoining brick.**

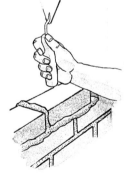

◀ **Using the trowel handle, tap the brick into place.**

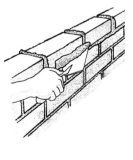

▶ **Scrape away any surplus mortar to leave the surfaces of the bricks and joints level.**

the second course are placed on whole bricks on the course below. This means that the vertical joints will align on alternate courses, and the easiest bond to start with is stretcher bond.

To lay **stretcher bond**, start by spreading a 10mm (⅜in) thick layer of mortar along the top of the first course of bricks, and drag the tip of your trowel through the mortar to create a slight furrow.

Start the second course by using a half-brick, then follow the same procedure for laying the second course of bricks as for the first, finishing with a half-brick.

Continue to lay courses of bricks in this way, but check that the wall is accurate, both horizontally and vertically, by using a spirit level at regular intervals.

BRICKLAYING: CHECKING VERTICAL AND HORIZONTAL PLANES

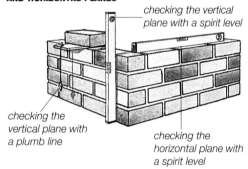

checking the vertical plane with a spirit level

checking the vertical plane with a plumb line

checking the horizontal plane with a spirit level

Cutting bricks

Regardless of which bonding pattern you use, it is inevitable that at some point you will have to cut bricks in half. This is usually done using a club hammer and a broad-bladed bolster chisel. Use the chisel to mark a line across the brick at the point where you intend to cut. Stand the brick on a firm, flat surface, and position the chisel on the marked line. Strike the top of the chisel firmly with the club hammer to break the brick.

Brick jointing and pointing

The type of joint used on a section of wall or other type of brickwork can have quite an effect on the overall final appearance. Therefore, careful consideration must be given when deciding the choice of joint. These joints are not just important for the sake of appearances but do have a considerable role to play in helping the wall to shed water.

The most commonly seen joints are:

(A) FLUSH

Here the joint mortar finishes flush with the brick face of the wall. This finish is excellent for exposed patio walls, there being no ledges in which water can settle.

(B) WEATHER STRUCK

Here, the mortar is impressed with a trowel so that an angle is formed which runs downwards and outwards. This starts approximately 5mm (¼in) in at the top of the joint, and slopes outwards to be flush with the wall face at the bottom. This is good for assisting rainwater to run downwards and away from the wall's face.

(C) BUCKET HANDLE

A gentle concave depression imparted into the mortar, originally achieved by drawing a bent bucket handle along the wet mortar. Now there is a specially designed tool bearing the name, although many landscapers prefer to use a 15cm (6in) length of hosepipe, which works just as well.

(D) KEYED

Here, the impression in the mortar is a more dramatic concave. In times past, a large key barrel would have

been used but today, a piece of piping does the same job, provided the diameter of it is only just larger that the width of the joint, to obtain the maximum possible depression.

(E) RECESSED

This method is used to push the wet mortar well back into the joint to finish squarely, and it obtains the most dramatic effect. This joint is, unfortunately, unsuitable for exposed sites, as water would collect on the ledges and might be driven into the wall.

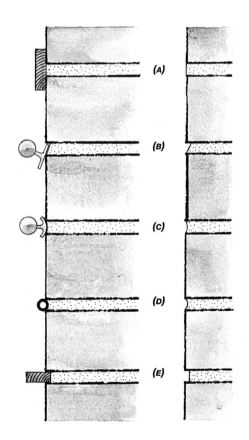

Gravel

Stones, whatever their size, can be used in a design to perform a similar task to grass or water. They can be made to 'flow' through the design, and link all its different aspects together. They form the open space which is so necessary to complement the plantings.

Self-binding gravel is a naturally occurring material and consists of particles which vary in size from 2 to 15mm. This is spread in layers, and needs to be wetted and compacted. In order to do this and get a firm even surface, a heavy hand-roller, mechanical vibrating roller, or mechanical compactor (whacker plate) should be used. The final depth of gravel after compaction should be between 25mm and 50mm, depending largely on the amount of use the area will be subject to. The finished surface should be even, but when used to surface a path, it is often laid with a camber (slightly raised in the centre or to one side) in order to help shed surface rainwater quickly and reduce the chance of algae, moss and lichen colonizing the gravel.

Gravel paths look better and last longer if they have an edging board, so that the sides are contained and cannot spread out into the surrounding soil. The self-binding type of gravel path needs to be checked annually, preferably in the spring after the hard frosts have passed, as frost often makes the top layer of gravel lift and work loose. Part of this annual maintenance usually involves the gravel being re-raked and re-rolled as necessary.

Continuous heavy use can also disrupt the surface and cause holes or irregularities, such as ruts. However, if well laid and regularly maintained, self-binding gravel will provide a firm, long-lasting surface for pedestrian use.

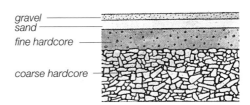

▲ **Spreading and levelling a gravel path before compaction.**

Yellow gravel was used in four gardens (Berkshire, Nottinghamshire, Camberwell and the Cotswolds) to form a firm, all-weather surface. It was laid, compacted with a motorized vibrating plate, thoroughly drenched with water, and compacted again to give a firm surface.

The hardness of this surface is due to the many different particle sizes of gravel being washed and settled by the water. They then bind together when the pressure of the vibrating plate is applied.

Gravel was also used as a mulch in the Camberwell garden, to give the impression of the plants having actually colonized the garden rather than it being a contrived planting scheme. The lighter-coloured gravels make perfect mulches to reflect sunlight and retain moisture, thus reducing the need for watering. These reflective qualities are ideal for making the best use of available light in a shaded situation, as in the Berkshire garden.

Wood

Timber is a warm, natural material which has a multitude of uses in the garden. It is hard-wearing, weather-resistant (more so if it is treated to prolong its life), and can be used to hold supports as the plants grow. Its main advantage is that it is so versatile; you can make almost anything from it, either from a kit or from scatch. For most simple structures, you do not need to be a carpenter, just have the appropriate tools and a modicum of common sense.

Wood totally dominated the Norwich garden, where the seating consisted of reclaimed timber, the boundary fence enclosing part of the garden was of chestnut poles, and even the paving was made from old railway sleepers (which make a safer surface for children than paving or bricks, as there is less chance of serious injury when slipping or falling).

The most difficult task within this garden was to

THE SIX-POLE WIGWAM

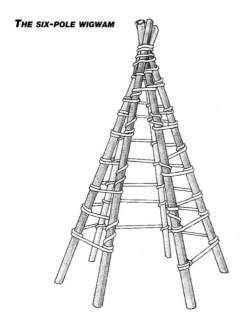

erect the wigwam, with each heavy pole being 5.5m (17ft) long (see opposite page).

In the Camberwell garden, the central area was dominated by a large wooden table, made from heavy-duty planks, with a bench seat along either side and was actually built on site by a team of joiners.

In the coastal gardens in Cornwall and Sussex and the material was in keeping with the surrounding area, being reclaimed timber which had previously been used to form part of the local sea defences.

In order to support the earth dam which would allow the construction of terracing at the garden in Sussex, the upright supports had to be cut to length and inserted about 1m (3ft) into the ground. In order to stabilize the base of each post on the shingle bank, four barrow-loads of a dry cement/shingle mix were placed around the bottom of the post; this would then gradually set as it attracted water from the surrounding soil/shingle. These posts were all positioned during the first day, and allowed to 'set' in place overnight. The following day horizontal planks were nailed into position, on the lower side of the slope. Sheets of marine plywood (placed behind the recycled timber to retain the soil) were then nailed to the planking; these broad sections of fabricated wood helped to even out the pressure along the entire terrace. They also gave us the opportunity to provide extra fastening to the horizontal planks of the terrace against the plywood, giving extra support. Many of the planks were split or had holes in them from bolts being removed when they were dismantled along the seafront, and the use of plywood acted as a barrier to stop soil and shingle spilling out of these holes. Very few fastenings were needed to hold these planks and the plywood in place; most of the support came from the pressure of the imported soil firmly packed against the planking, pushing it against the upright posts.

Constructing a Wigwam

1 Each of the six poles had a 10mm (⅜in)hole drilled through it, at a distance of 75cm (2½ft) from one end.

2 Three of the posts were fixed together at the top of their length with strong thin wire hawser threaded through holes drilled in each pole. This was done while they were still laid on the ground.

3 A sturdy rope was then tied to the top of the middle one of the three poles so that they could be hauled upright.

4 The poles were opened up to form an 'A' frame (two poles forming one leg and one forming the other).

5 With two people pulling on the rope and one person on each leg to steady the frame, we pulled the 'A' frame into an upright position.

6 When the poles were roughly upright we then separated the two poles forming one leg, to open out the structure into a tripod.

7 Each pole was buried 45cm (18in) into the ground to make it stable, with the base of each pole being firmly placed on a piece of paving slab to prevent any sinkage.

8 After the tripod was firmly in position and safe, the three remaining poles were added to the structure and the base of each of these additional poles was firmly placed on a piece of paving slab to prevent any sinkage and the holes filled with soil.

9 Using a ladder we climbed up the structure and all six poles were wired into place.

With safety in mind, the frame was actually erected up the slope of the garden, which allowed total control of the situation and greatly reduced the chances of anyone getting injured.

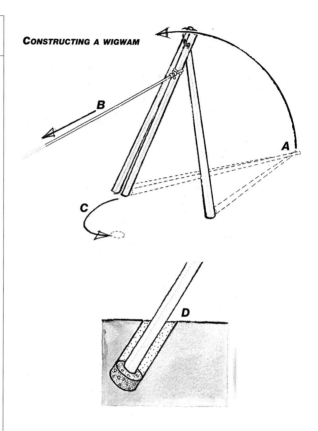

CONSTRUCTING A WIGWAM

B

A

C

D

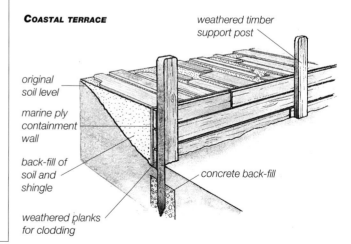

COASTAL TERRACE

weathered timber
support post

original
soil level

marine ply
containment
wall

back-fill of
soil and
shingle

concrete back-fill

weathered planks
for clodding

▲ *Slatted decking is perfect for a seating area.*

Decking

Timber decking is popular as a hard surface in warm, dry climates, but decks can be used anywhere provided that the timber used has been pressure-treated with a good preservative.

It is best to build the deck on a level or gently sloping site. For a raised deck on a steep, sloping site, it is advisable to seek specialist assistance, since it will need to be well designed and constructed.

In some countries there are building regulations which state that all exterior areas of decking must be able to support a stipulated minimum weight. It may also be necessary to obtain a building permit in some areas and have the work inspected. If in any doubt concerning the regulations, check with your local authority building department.

Simple parquet decking (or duckboarding) which is laid on gravel and sand should not require permission.

Slatted decking is suitable for level or gently sloping ground. It is simple to install, and requires few special fittings.

▶ *Raised decking can be used as a garden feature as well as having a practical use on a sloping site.*

DECKING

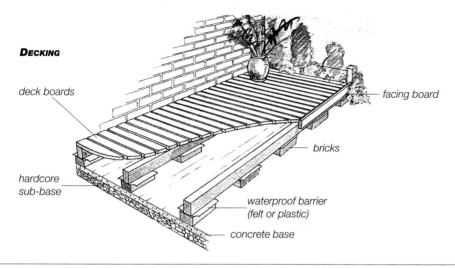

deck boards

facing board

bricks

hardcore
sub-base

waterproof barrier
(felt or plastic)

concrete base

Building a deck

1 For an area close to a building such as a house, lay a concrete foundation. This should slope gently away from the building to make sure that any water drains away.

2 Lay a row of bricks on to the concrete base and mortar them into position. These should be spaced about one brick apart, and be at right angles to the intended direction of the decking planks.

3 These bricks should be laid in rows 45cm (18in) apart. As you work, keep checking that the bricks are level – this will make life easier later when laying down the supporting joists.

4 Lay 75mm x 50mm (3in x 2in) joists over the bricks, inserting a damp-proof material between the bricks and the joists. If you are joining lengths of timber together, make sure there is a brick support beneath the point where the joists meet and screw a piece of wood or a metal bracket across the joist. (As you work, check the levels between joists using a spirit level and a straight edge.)

5 When the joists are fixed into position, lay the deck planks at right angles to the joists. These are usually 75 x 25mm (3 x 1in) in size. Allow 10mm (⅜in) gaps between the planks for free drainage and to allow some movement of the timber as it swells or shrinks in response to changing weather conditions. Ensure that joints in the decking planks are staggered from row to row and that the planks are butt-jointed (ends flush) over a supporting joist.

6 Secure the decking planks with nails or screws (brass or some other rustproof metal is ideal). When using screws, countersink them to a level beneath the upper surface of the planks.

7 These holes can be topped up with a wood filler which closely matches the colour of the wood.

8 Finish the deck with a length of facing timber which can be screwed or nailed along the cut edges.

PARQUET DECKING

It is possible to purchase small, parquet-type, timber squares, which are intended primarily for use as paths, but can also be used for decking. Alternatively, they can be home-made quite easily. To lay these, prepare a base on firmed ground or subsoil with 7.5cm (3in) of compacted gravel topped with 7.5cm (3in) of sand. Level and compact the sand before laying the squares in alternate directions, and when they are in their final positions, nail the squares together to stop them moving. Drive the nails in at an angle, to get a firmer grip into the wood.

Decking can also be used to create an unusual 'stepping-stone' style of path across a pond. They can add a geometric element to the informal planting and soft play of light on and around a pond or similar water feature.

Many people shy away from the use of timber decking because they believe that wood will quickly rot, but if it is treated with the correct type of preservative, it can have a useful life expectancy of at least twenty-five years. Always use treated wood where possible, 'tannalized' for preference, and apply a preservative or stain on an annual basis to get the best results from the timber you use. It is best to use microporous stains, which allow any moisture in the wood to escape; if trapped beneath an impermeable layer, it will eventually cause the coloured surface layer to lift. All wooden surfaces for staining should be dry and free from dirt. Always read the instructions on the container, and follow when using any form of wood treatment.

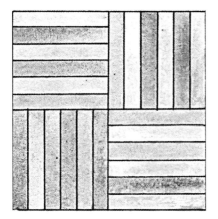

PARQUET

Wattle

Using traditional skills, this natural material can be made into fences, gardening furniture and sculptures. In recent years, it has gained a great deal of popularity as a construction component for sculpted figures. In the Norwich garden, a child's cave-like shelter was made of woven wattle, a hurdle which had been bent into a curved shape. The Cotswolds garden design was dominated by wattle, with gates, fences and a raised bank (or 'Cornish hedge') being constructed from it.

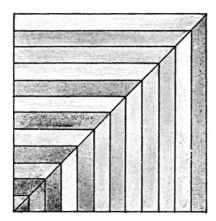

CONCENTRIC RECTANGLE

Making a 'Cornish hedge'

1   We drove support posts into the soil to a depth of 75cm (2½ft) to hold the hurdles in place. These were positioned in such a way as to form a narrow alley of 60cm (2ft) wide.

2   Sheets of marine-grade plywood 75cm (2½ft) deep were fastened to the outsides of the posts with nails (this would act as a lining to prevent any soil spilling out through the gaps in the hurdles).

3   The hurdles were then fastened to the outside of the ply, and fixed with wire loops which went through the plywood and around the posts behind them.

4   The 60cm (2ft) wide, 75cm (2½ft) deep alley between the hurdles was then filled with soil to create the earth bank for the hedge to grow in. The larger wattle panels were used as fencing panels and erected between firmly positioned posts.

Metal

Apart from the obvious materials such as screws, nails and hinges etc., metal only really featured in four gardens. The Camberwell garden had a prefabricated arbour made of metal box-sections, assembled on site, and the Balham garden used copper tubing as upright supports for the pergola. The Herne Hill project, however (it is difficult to think of it as a conventional garden) was totally dominated by metal. A long metal cage had to be constructed and fixed to the outside of the balcony on each floor of this building to hold the planting troughs. Inside these metal cages, galvanized steel troughs 30cm (12in) wide, 40cm (16in) deep and over 5m (15ft) long were placed (three on each balcony).

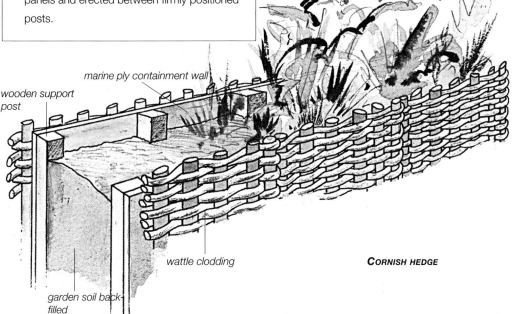

wooden support post

marine ply containment wall

wattle clodding

garden soil back-filled

CORNISH HEDGE

◄ *A metal framework will provide support for climbing plants which will eventually shade this seating area.*

the metal hoops, running horizontally along the length of the archway to give the structure strength and rigidity.

In order to make height adjustment and levelling easier, we hammered 45cm (18in) long metal tubes into the ground. These were 23mm diameter, so that the base of each hoop slotted into the tube. This stopped the legs of the hoops springing out of the ground due to the tension created when the hoops were bent over to form the arch.

Lighting

Don't overlook night-time in the garden. This is when most entertaining occurs, and for most gardeners it is the only time they may spend in their garden during the week. So obviously the garden should look special. A series of strategically placed lights to emphasize the largest or most choice plants in the garden and any outstanding features can make a well-cared-for garden look even better.

Garden lighting can be divided into two main categories:

- **Practical lighting**, for use in safety and security, areas such as drives, paths, pools, seats, steps and terraces.
- **Ornamental lighting** for amenity value, beauty and interest. Garden features such as arches, walls, statues and stonework, and plants such as trees, shrubs and conifers can all provide an extra dimension to the garden when lit at night. Whenever possible, combine the two types of lighting to provide both function and beauty.

The second visit to Sarah and Oliver's Buckinghamshire garden saw the use of metal to form the apple arch. This arch was constructed from 13mm mild-steel rods, bent over to give a span of 2.4m (8ft) wide and about 2.5m (8½ft) high at the ridge. The rods were bent by hand into a rough semi-circle, but we left the ends of the rods wider apart than the intended width of the arch. This meant that when the hoops were positioned, they were held in place by the tension of the bent steel rods. The total structure consisted of 8 hoops, positioned at 1m (3ft) spacings. The rods were drilled at intervals, and five metal tie-straps were bolted to the outside edge of

The need for practical lighting is always much easier to determine; ornamental lighting is much more a matter of personal preference or can be omitted from a garden entirely.

With garden lighting, you are dealing with lamps rather than bulbs, and many of these come as complete sealed (waterproof units).

Up-lighting

Usually this is using light from ground level, shining upwards, and tends to be most effective at the base of the object be featured. Usually the light source is placed in front of the object to be lit, and it is very effective when used on the white stems of birch or eucalyptus. The light could be placed behind the object, to create an interesting silhouette on a subject such as a specimen tree. The main problem is in placing the light so that it cannot be seen directly, but shines on the object to be illuminated. With larger trees, cross-lights are placed at either side of the tree, aimed directly into the canopy, with a third up-light placed in front of the tree shining up the stem.

Down-lighting

This is lighting directed downwards. It can be positioned above, below, or at, eye level. The larger the area to be covered, the higher the position of the light must be, but the problem of glare is encountered as soon as eye level is reached. However, this problem can be solved with the careful placement of the lamps, and the use of shields or filters.

Any electrical fixtures and fittings intended for use outdoors must be well-made and waterproof, and the hidden light source, although it does not need to be an attractive design, should be compact and

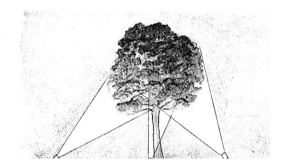

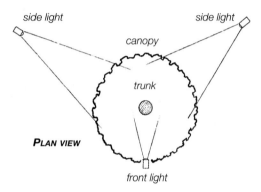

▲ *The use of up-lighting from ground level: position side lights to up-light the tree canopy; direct the front light at the trunk to emphasise its colour and shape.*

functional. When the fixture is visible, it should be of a size and design appropriate to the setting in which it is to be placed.

For safety reasons, 90 per cent of all garden lighting is low-voltage (12 volts), coming through a transformer from the mains power supply. This has many advantages over high-voltage systems, and the effect is usually more subtle. According to many of the manufacturers of garden lighting, no special tools

▲ Downlighting: the larger the area to be covered, the higher the position of the lights. For a moonlighting effect, lights should be placed high up in trees to shine down through leaves, creating patterns on the ground below.

or skills are required to install low-voltage lights. Wires can be buried 15cm (5in) deep, hung on a wall or fence or laid on the surface where they are not likely to be severed with any garden implements (organic mulch is a perfect camouflage for low-voltage wires). Because they require no conduit, cables can be moved easily until the best effect is achieved. They can be added to gardens with quite established plantings, causing very little disturbance.

After planning, construction and planting in a garden have been completed, the final positioning of garden lights should be done at night to get the exact effect required. Some experts advise working with extension cords, shifting fittings around until the desired effect is achieved. One of the best ways to avoid damaging plants is to install most of the system before planting, and to use plug-in type fixtures on short cords.

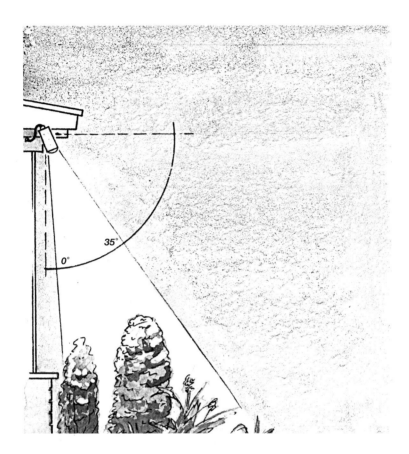

Costs vary considerably for the installation of garden lighting and individual fittings, and any electrical work involving a mains supply must be carried out by a qualified electrician and often requires inspection.

In order to save costs, it is possible for you to dig trenches and do the other preparation before the contractor comes in to do the lighting and electrical installation, as we did in the restaurant garden at Crouch End.

▲ *To minimise glare, a down-light should be angled within 0° to 35° above the plants to lit. This type of lighting is also an excellent security feature, to deter intruders. Only low-voltage lighting is used for safety reasons.*

Soft Landscaping

4

A garden needs to be designed around the amount of time which will be put into it, and this is the first consideration when approaching soft landscaping. A low-maintenance scheme means that there will be time to spend elsewhere in the garden, and involves simple options that make all the difference: an alternative ground-cover scheme instead of a lawn, self-supporting climbers rather than a time-consuming hedge.

The next stage is to decide upon an appropriate theme. In Sarah and Oliver's case the theme was a managed wild garden designed to reflect the Buckinghamshire countryside, and we had to choose plants that were entirely in keeping with that concept, varieties that felt wild even though they were garden selections, such as the purple-leaved form of our native elder. For the Crouch End restaurant, WXD, the planting revolved around the decision to choose an eclectic mix of plants which were all edible and combine them in a way that would make them look fun and exciting.

The garden should be a reflection of its owner or of the people who are living and working in it. If a relationship is not established between the two, the garden will fail to evolve and develop a spirit of its own. Once the theme has been decided, the choice of plants should be brainstormed together. An initial broad list should be compiled, divided

▶ **Agapanthus *'Isis', ragweed and Stipa tenuissima *in the background.**

up into trees, shrubs, perennials, ground cover, climbers and so on. You may have very particular preferences in terms of taste, and this will come through during the brainstorming session. Reference books and magazines are ideal sources of information, and looking at what is growing in nearby gardens is often a great help. You may favour hot saturated colour or more subtle cooler tones; you may prefer plants with a relaxed feel to them, like those we used in the Camberwell garden; or you may want more of a sense of order and architecture. These are all important considerations at the outset.

When selecting plants it is important to consider once again the practicalities of your site. If, like Meri in Berkshire, you have very little sunshine, there is no point including sun-loving lavender, for instance. With Wendy and Leslie's garden in Sussex, conditions dictated to such an extent that initially it looked as if the choice of material would be limited. The community garden in Nottinghamshire demanded a range of plants which, in contrast to those in Judy and Ciarán's Gulf-Stream garden in Cornwall, would have to endure the harshness of poor soil coupled with a climate which was cold in winter and dry in summer. With a comprehensive plant knowledge and an understanding of your limitations you can create a successful garden – choosing the right plant for the right place is really half the battle.

The final stage of plant selection is to prune the list which you put together at the brainstorming session and which may well have been considerably reduced when climatic and site considerations were evaluated. The final selection should include the best and most appropriate from the list, dividing the selection into framework plants, fill-in plants and understory plants and climbers.

The framework plants will include larger shrubs, to add height and bulk, and trees if your garden is large enough. The choice of trees should be made very carefully: they must be appropriate for the site not only aesthetically but also, and more importantly, in terms of size. Many trees which look wonderful in the nursery or as an image at the back of your mind may, in fact, grow too big for your garden, and there is nothing more frustrating or more time-consuming than having to prune a tree or even remove it because it is in the wrong place.

(Trees should also be carefully placed so that they do not overhang buildings, neighbours or planting schemes.) It is a lot more difficult to remove a tree than to plant one.

Shrubs provide the secondary framework of a garden. Evergreens are necessary for winter interest and also for their value as screening plants, breaking up long lines of fencing or creating a sense of intrigue by making it impossible to see the garden all at once. Coupling the evergreens with deciduous species is necessary in order to achieve seasonal variety and a lightness which can often be lacking in schemes dominated by evergreens.

The third part of the framework is the hedging material. This can be used as a division within the garden, to hide an eyesore, or to make a screen for privacy. In Andy and Louise's garden in the Cotswolds we replaced the scruffy lonicera hedge with a piebald mix of copper and green beech to give a more interesting back to a border. We also replaced their privet hedge, which would have taken several cuts a year to keep in trim, with a native hedge which could grow to its natural size and blend in more effectively with the surrounding countryside.

Hedges and structure planting can also be used for protection from the elements. The subtropical garden planted in the lower part of Judy and Ciarán's garden in Cornwall would certainly not have survived if we had not retained the old established escallonia. If there had not been adequate wind protection already there, we would have had to plant shelter shrubs and wait for them to grow before being able to plant more exotic species. This structure planting is all important in a garden. It will create the mood, the physical divisions and the framework for other plantings to come and go over the seasons.

The fill-in plants will include perennials, grasses and bulbs, plants which are transitory throughout the seasons and which may well be the elements which introduce colour and accent into the garden. In Meri's garden in Berkshire we chose a range of shade-tolerant perennials with pale flowers to provide a lift in the low light levels; in Robin's garden in Balham the perennials were themed so that rich dark saturated colours dominated the scheme. Interplanted among the shrubby material they provided seasonal variety in the garden, flowering in succession so that in the relatively small space there was always something of interest.

Choosing a range of perennials which follow on from one another throughout the year will help to maintain interest. It is important to consider the quieter times in the garden, such as the early spring and the late summer and autumn, so that there is always something to look forward to. A garden which performs in one great flurry may well leave you disappointed for the rest of the year. The perennials in the community garden in Nottinghamshire were the element of the garden designed to take over from the winter framework of trees and shrubs. Once again they were staggered so that they took over after the June blossom of elder and pyracantha. Choosing perennials which do not require staking, such as the self-supporting achilleas and sedums, will save time.

Many are quite happy to be left alone for several years without division, which is a labour-saving consideration at selection time.

Prolonging the season of interest with perennials is easily done by selecting varieties which dry well in winter, such as the rudbeckias, *Sedum* 'Autumn Joy' and the sea-thistles. Their winter skeletons will provide you with a frame for winter frost and form which on closer examination is infinitely better than bare soil. There is a wealth of perennials available which have been selected over the years for their endurance and out-of-season interest. Choosing a considered selection over the traditional choice of lupins and delphiniums will lift the garden to another level.

The ornamental grasses are becoming increasingly popular, and can be used to give lightness and softness to a perennial scheme. They are an ideal foil for both flowers and foliage, and when repeated through a garden bring continuity to a scheme. They should not be overlooked for fear of their weedy associations. Many will live quite happily in one place, pushing through bright in the spring and remaining as bleached and wiry forms in the winter. Although not always appropriate for every scheme, there is a large enough range of good varieties that can be adapted to most situations.

The bulbs do not necessarily need to be planted in the first phase of the plans, but with their ability to push through other low-growing perennials to add a seasonal lift and unexpected association, they should be included in the great scheme of things. Many of the bulbs are those we associate with spring. They will pull the garden interest forward by at least a month. Others, however, such as the ornamental onions, are ideal for interplanting among plants such as iris and shrub roses to add another layer of interest

through a planting scheme.

The ground-coverers should be part of every garden. Their ground-hugging growth will smother competition from weeds and provide a layer of interest underneath trees and shrubs; they are an essential element of every garden, a green and protecting eiderdown. A well-planted scheme will be much easier to look after than a lawn or borders with bare soil. Many are evergreen and tolerant of considerable shade and drought, the ideal companions for shrubs. Others are tolerant of sun and drought and are perfect plants for the front of the border. Planted among more ephemeral perennials, they will lessen the amount of ground to be weeded and protect the soil, maintaining moisture and actively adding to the humus levels with their continual growth and decomposition.

The fourth group, the climbers, are worthy of consideration for their ability to rise above the shade at ground level, to cover unsightly objects and to blur boundaries when planted along perimeter fences and walls. The choice is wide: there are varieties which are suitable for sun and for shade. Choice of self-clinging or twining species will be one of the main considerations. Although the self-clingers such as *Hydrangea petiolaris* and Virginia creeper may well need initial help to get them attached, once away they will provide their own support. The twiners, such as wisteria, vines and clematis, will need a structure such as a trellis or wires or the framework of another shrub as a support and will initially need tying in.

◀ *Bergamot and bronze fennel in the Norwich garden: a semi-transparent screen to soften the wooden fencing.*
▼ *Planting creating the contours of the gravel path leading to the arbour in the Camberwell garden. A mix of shrubs and perennials provides constant change and interest.*

Without such an aid they will writhe around in a confusion at ground level.

Careful consideration should be given to climbers. Like your choice of trees and shrubs, mistakes can easily be made by choosing an over-vigorous species for a confined situation. Mile-a-minute, *Polygonum baldschuanicum*, is not misnamed, and you should certainly think twice about rambling roses such as 'Kiftsgate' which have the potential to take over the whole garden.

Climbers should only ever be planted into a shrub or tree if the support is well enough developed. They can easily strangle something if it is not equipped to deal with the extra weight and bulk of a climber. Having said that, climbers are ideal associates for shrubs such as philadelphus or lilac, which bloom early and then tend to look rather dull for the rest of the season. A climber can bring life to hidden corners and elevate the garden up on to the vertical plane. Although they can be considerably time-consuming to maintain, when well chosen they should be an element of every garden.

Plant association is like the icing on the cake. Good combinations can create virtually maintenance-free areas of your garden, if that is what is required. They can be the lift that a garden needs to make it special and they can provide the friction needed for essential vitality. It may take years to learn about the best associations, but one helpful rule is to choose plants which are compatible, meaning that they both require the same conditions in terms of soil type, light and tolerance of exposure. They must also be good companions, one not being more vigorous than the other.

An unbalanced scheme will result in continual maintenance in an attempt to readjust that balance. An equilibrium is what one should be looking for. The old-style traditional herbaceous border is a high-maintenance element in a garden, mainly because of the wildly differing habits of the plants involved. The most effective planting schemes pay attention to the requirements of a plant first, placing aesthetic considerations second.

When planning your planting scheme, the most effective course of action is to start with the key plants first, the shrubs or trees or, in the case of perennial schemes, the most dominant plants on the list. These plants will give the scheme a flavour and theme. Choosing a limited range of plants and using them in large numbers will give a scheme a much needed continuity. If these simple rules are followed, detail and embellishment can be added at a later date.

The maxim 'less is more' is worth remembering. It will be the route to a scheme which is both restful and balanced. In Camberwell, for example, we divided the garden into three main areas – shade, sun and planting in areas of gravel. This established the groups for compatibility first. Next the lists were put together to include the key plants for each area, such as the bamboo in the shade and the buddleja and cortaderia in the gravel. In each situation the planting was then broken down into several dominant plants, such as the horizontal achillea and sedum which we knew were comparable in terms of growth rate.

These drifts were then broken up with vertical accent plants, the grasses, working down to the details, the self-seeding eschscholzias and small groups of brightly-coloured cranesbill in the nooks around the perimeter of the garden. Attention was paid first to compatibility, second to detail, the best path to a scheme which will endure both in terms of interest and longevity.

Soil preparation

Soil preparation usually involves various methods of soil cultivation, including weed control, digging, and adding soil improvers, and is vital to successful long-term plant growth. Weeds compete with cultivated plants for space, light, nutrients, and water – in fact, all the essentials for strong healthy growth. They may

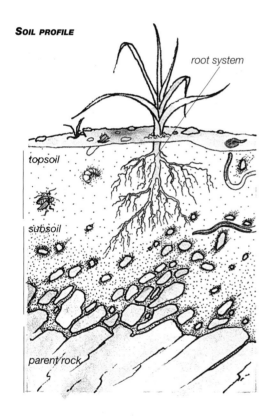

SOIL PROFILE

root system

topsoil

subsoil

parent rock

▲ **The top-soil zone is the most biologically-active region in a soil profile.**

also harbour diseases, which makes their eradication or control vital. Different digging techniques are used to cultivate the soil in different ways, depending on its condition and the plants to be grown.

If the condition of the soil is poor, it may be improved by adding organic material, usually at the same time as digging. The top 30cm (1ft) of the soil (topsoil) is the most biologically active and this is the area where organic matter should be incorporated to have the most beneficial effect.

The aim is always to create a soil which holds moisture but is free-draining, and one which encourages the types of soil organism which help to maintain fertility in the root zone of the plants. Some soil-borne organisms are essential for maintaining soil fertility. Many beneficial bacteria and fungi thrive in a well-drained soil and can tolerate a wide range of soil pH. Small insects and mites play a vital part in the breakdown of organic matter within the soil, and creatures such as earthworms feeding and burrowing in the soil have the effect of improving both the soil structure and its drainage system.

Soil pH

This is the expression of the soil's acidity or alkalinity, measured on a scale ranging from 1 to 14, with neutral being the mid-point (pH 7.0). A pH reading of below 7.0 is an indication that the soil sample is acidic, with a reading over 7.0 indicating an alkaline (chalky) soil sample. An important part of soil preparation is to test the soil pH, as this will often indicate the plants you can grow, and the type of organic material which should be used to improve the soil.

Testing soil pH

You can check on the pH of your soil to determine its acidity by using a soil-testing kit. In the *Garden Doctors* series we tested the soil to gain more information about the range of plants we could introduce into a client's garden. Small versions of these test kits are readily available from garden centres, and it takes only a few minutes to discover whether or not your soil is suitable for certain plants. As a rough guide, if your soil measures more than 6.5 on the pH scale, it is unsuitable for growing acid-lovers, such as rhododendrons, azaleas or pieris. Of course, even if this is the case, you can always grow them in containers on the terrace or patio, where you have complete control over the growing medium.

Remember, soil pH is not always directly linked to soil type. Acid soils can be free-draining and sandy, heavy and sticky, or organic with a high peat content. Clay soils may be acid or alkaline, depending on their make-up, but tend to be of a much more consistent nature, as they are less affected by rainwater leaching out lime than acid sandy soils. We found the soil in parts of Meri and Dick's Berkshire garden to be slightly alkaline, but very stony and free-draining.

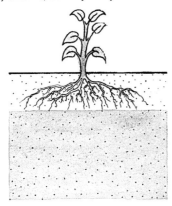

▲ *A high water table restricts root development.*

The effects of pH

The correct term for plants which prefer to grow in an alkaline soil (with a pH of 7.0 or higher) is calcicoles. Plants growing in this type of soil can have problems with nutrient deficiency, because at a pH of about 7.5, potash and manganese start to become much less available to the plants. The availability of phosphate, iron and boron starts to decline, too, so that above pH 8.0, all are in short supply.

At the other end of the scale there is a great deal of confusion over the terminology used to describe plants which prefer to grow in an acid soil. They are often wrongly referred to as ericaceous plants, because many acid-loving plants belong to the family Ericaceae, including such subjects as erica, pieris and rhododendron. It is well worth remembering that many other ornamental plants, such as camellia, hamamelis and some magnolias, are also acid-loving but are not of the family Ericaceae. The correct term for plants which prefer acid soil is calcifuges.

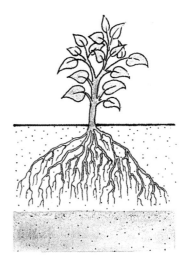

▲ *Well-drained soil lowers the water table and allows deeper rooting.*

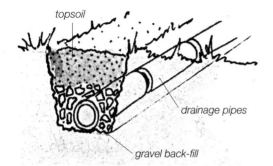

topsoil

drainage pipes

gravel back-fill

◀ *To improve drainage on sites where the water table is high, install an underground drainage system. On sloping ground, lay the drains to run parallel to the soil level.*

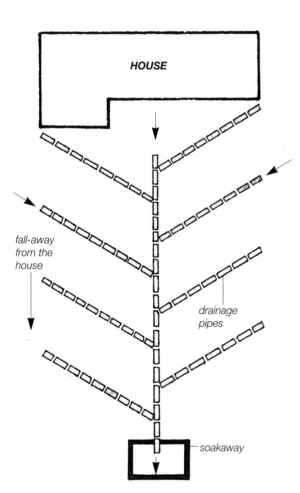

HOUSE

fall-away from the house

drainage pipes

soakaway

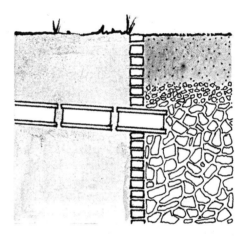

◀ *(Left and above)* **Install drains about 60cm below soil-level, and have them leading to a ditch or soakaway.**

Planting

Most gardeners already know that spring and autumn are the best times for planting, but this does not mean that planting at any other time is not possible, and certainly not now that most of the plants we buy are grown in containers. The major advantage of container-grown plants is that they may be bought and planted at any time of year, so it is possible to purchase shrubs in full leaf and flower and successfully establish them. The key to successful planting is to ensure the plants are well planted and cared for until they have fully established.

The planting hole for a tree or shrub must be large enough to accommodate the root system without it having to be trimmed. Before planting is even considered, check the moisture level of the rootball. If it appears dry, give it a good watering or stand the whole root system in a container such as a bucket of water, to soak it thoroughly.

If the plant is container-grown, make sure that the planting hole is about twice the diameter of the present container and slightly deeper than its depth. The base and sides of the hole should be broken up with a fork to encourage root growth into the surrounding soil.

After preparing the planting hole, remove the surface compost from the top 2.5cm (1in) of the rootball in the pot, where any dormant weed seeds may be. Most of us have quite enough weeds of our own already. After the plant has been correctly positioned, backfill the hole with a mixture of soil and bulky organic matter such as well-rotted compost or farmyard manure. After filling the hole with the planting mixture, carefully firm the soil around the plant using the heel of a boot, or for smaller plants, the hand.

Bare-root trees

Trees sold bare-root, which are almost always deciduous, are grown in open ground (a nursery field). They are lifted in the autumn/winter with virtually no soil around the roots, and it is essential to buy them when they are dormant, from autumn through to early spring. Birch (*Betula*), poplars (*Populus*), and many native trees, such as alder (*Alnus*), hawthorn (*Crataegus*) and oak (*Quercus*) are often sold bare-root in a range of sizes. Many of these were planted in the community garden in Nottinghamshire.

Make sure that the tree you choose has well-developed roots spreading evenly in all directions. Examine the roots to check that they are free from damage and disease and that there is no sign of dryness that may have been caused by exposure to wind. As the root system of a newly planted tree will take a number of growing seasons to anchor firmly in the soil, staking may be necessary initially, especially for larger trees.

Staking

A low stake is now often preferred, as it allows the tree to move naturally in the wind but keeps the root system firmly anchored. This method uses a vertical stake, placed on the side of the prevailing wind and long enough to reach to 15cm (6in) above soil level. The stake must be driven in about 75cm (30in) below soil level so that it is firmly fixed and completely stable. This stake must be inserted as the tree is planted, not driven into the ground after planting, as it could cause damage to the roots.

For container-grown and rootballed trees, a low stake angled into the prevailing wind may be preferable as it can be driven in clear of the rootball even after the tree has been planted.

Another method of helping the tree to establish quickly is to reduce the length of the branches.In the community garden in Nottinghamshire, we did not stake the young white poplars (*Populus alba*) but pruned all the branches back to 10cm (4in) from the main stem. This cuts down wind-resistance, allowing the roots to take hold, and reduces the leaf area of the tree in the first spring after planting, which in turn reduces moisture stress.

Aftercare

The key elements to successful planting are:

- Firm planting.
- Watering.
- Mulching.

The compost, which contains most of the roots, can dry out much more quickly than the surrounding soil, so be prepared to water regularly, especially in sandy soils, and never rely on summer rainfall to provide enough water for newly planted shrubs. Make sure that the top of the compost is about 2.5cm (1in) below the final soil level after planting. This will prevent the compost being exposed to the air, and reduce the chance of it drying out. If this is allowed to happen, then the rootball will dry and shrink away from the sides of the planting hole, and the plant will almost certainly die.

Improve moisture retention by adding plenty of organic matter. Apply soluble fertilizers little and often, up to three or four times during the growing season, or, even better, mix a slow-release fertilizer as a top-dressing immediately after planting.

When planting, create a small depression around the stem of the plant, to act as a reservoir to hold water where it is most needed. This was a technique we used in Nottinghamshire, where parts of the garden were on a dry sloping site. Finally, apply enough mulch to cover an area at least twice the diameter of the planting hole. This mulch should be at least 5cm (2in) thick.

Plants which have been placed in exposed positions, as in Leslie and Wendy's coastal garden in Sussex, may need some protection from drying winds. This can be achieved quite easily by erecting a barrier of fleece or netting to act as windbreak for up to six weeks after planting. You can regularly drench the foliage by spraying over with water to cut down the water lost by evaporation, and water heavily and regularly rather than little and often.

All these measures are rather pointless if you start with poor-quality plants in the first place. If at all possible, always inspect the plants thoroughly before you buy them. Look for good specimens with evenly distributed balanced growth, and choose plants which are accurately labelled and appear to be healthy, undamaged, and free from obvious signs of pests and diseases. Avoid plants which have a covering of weed on the compost surface, as it usually indicates that the plants have been on sale for a long time and have not been cared for particularly well.

If possible, inspect the plant's root system by sliding the plant out of its container. Look for a mass of firm, white-tipped roots (these are the new active feeding roots). Reject plants with poorly developed root systems and those which are pot-bound (filled with roots and hardly any compost left in the container, or thick roots circling inside the bottom of the pot), as these rarely establish well.

If there are roots growing out of the bottom of the

Slow-release fertilizers

These are sophisticated chemical formulations which have been designed to release nutrients slowly over a predictable period of time. They work by attracting water and then absorbing it until they are so full that a solution of water and fertilizer seeps out into the surrounding soil. This will happen over a period of many months or even years in some cases. The main advantage is that one application will feed the plant for quite a long time before a second application is required.

In most of the gardens, a liberal dressing of this controlled-release fertilizer was applied to the soil after planting. It was always broadcast (scattered) over the soil, and then lightly incorporated with a fork, to start the release of nutrients.

▲ *Pruning branches which have been broken down to the tree stem.*

container and you still want to buy the plant, be prepared to sacrifice the pot by cutting it away from the root system. This is a far better option than to run the risk of damaging the plant's roots by trying to slide the pot from the rootball.

Slow-release fertilizer

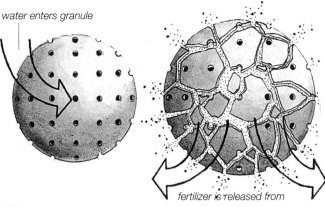

water enters granule

fertilizer is released from the splitting granule

▶ *Sometimes, the granule splits due to internal pressure and fertilizer is released into the surrounding soil. Usually, however, the granule remains intact and the fertilizer seeps out as a solution through the pores.*

Applying a fertilizer in this way has a number of advantages:

- It benefits the greatest area of soil.
- It reduces the risk of individual plants being damaged by over-feeding.
- As the nutrients are released, they percolate down through the soil to the area where the roots are ready to receive them.

After applying fertilizer in a broadcast fashion, always go round the garden tapping the plants with a cane to prevent any of the chemical pellets settling on the leaves and stems, where they can damage the plants by scorching them.

Mulching

Any material applied to the surface of the soil primarily to reduce the loss of water by evaporation or to control weeds may be termed a mulch.

Weed control: mulching can be an extremely effective method for the control of annual and perennial weeds, depending on the materials used.

Moisture conservation: a mulch of sufficient depth acts to limit the amount of water lost from the soil, and reduce the need for watering.

Temperature regulation: some mulches can be used to keep the soil cooler in the summer and warmer in the winter; as a consequence, the plant's roots and overall growth can benefit and an improvement in growth rate can be achieved.

Most organic mulches used to be applied to a minimum depth for them to be fully effective. With organic mulches such as shredded bark, a depth of 10cm (4in) is necessary for effective weed control, whereas a minimum depth of 5cm (2in) is adequate to dramatically reduce moisture loss from the soil's

surface. As many weed seeds will only germinate in the presence of light, the mulch has to be of sufficient depth to block out the light and prevent germination. The mulch will not kill the weed seeds but they will gradually deteriorate and die if they are under the mulch for a number of years.

Organic mulches such as shredded bark or wood chippings have the advantage of decomposing to provide an additional source of organic material. This in turn encourages the activity of bacteria, insects and worms. The combination of this added activity and the increased levels of organic material goes a long way to increasing soil fertility and consequently improving plant growth. The downside of this particular process is that the biodegradable organic matter will gradually decompose, so in order to maintain the correct depth of mulch, it will be

▼ *In the coastal garden, gravel was used to protect the soil from the effects of eroding winds and drying sunshine.*

necessary to top up the level every other year.

Some plants may show symptoms of nitrogen deficiency soon after a mulch has been applied. This is because woody mulches require a high level of bacterial activity to start rotting, and as bacterial activity is promoted by the nutrient nitrogen, the bacteria may 'borrow' the plants' available nitrogen from the soil. To overcome this, sprinkle 450g of nitrogen-based fertilizer over an area of 10sq m. This boost of nitrogen will prevent the plants becoming nitrogen deficient.

It is also important to use only composted materials: materials such as bark, manure, sawdust, wood chips and grass clippings generate very high temperatures as they decompose. If these materials are applied fresh, they can damage the very plants you wish to protect. Fresh bark from coniferous forests can be lethal to plants until it has been composted to remove traces of tarpenoid compounds which are toxic to plants.

Applying mulches

It must be remembered that any mulch is only as effective as the soil preparation which is carried out prior to its application. You must always remove all perennial weeds before adding the mulch, or these weeds will benefit from the effects of mulching every bit as much as the plants you are trying to help. Never apply mulches if the soil is waterlogged or frozen, or the insulating qualities of the mulch will act to keep the soil cold and wet for much longer than you would normally expect.

Many mulches are at their most effective when

▲ *This is an ideal method of retaining soil moisture and controlling annual weeds. The mulch should be applied up to the base of the plant.*

MULCHES

	AVAILABILITY	APPLICATION	DURABILITY	ADVANTAGES	DISADVANTAGES
Bark	Becoming available in many garden stores or direct from mills.	Shrubberies and borders.	Top up every 2 years.	Looks attractive and improves the structure of the soil.	Must be well fermented. Does not add nutrients.
Compost	Can be made in any garden.	Anywhere.	Renew annually.	Improves both the fertility of the soil and its structure.	Takes time and effort to make.
Creeping plants	Universal.	Beneath trees and shrubs.	Long-term, but can be wiped out rapidly by pests or disease.	The most attractive weed suppressant.	Takes a long time to become really effective.
Manure	Freely available in rural areas.	Anywhere.	Dissipates quickly.	Improves and enriches the soil	If not well rotted, it can be acid and smelly; it introduces weed seeds into the garden.
Peat	Available.	In shrubberies and in borders.	Loses roughly 15 per cent of its volume every year.	Improves soil structure. Looks good.	Blows about when dry.
Plastic sheet	Universal.	Shrubberies.	Long-term.	Excellent weed suppressant.	Unsightly and needs covering. Does not add nutrients.
Sawdust	Easy to obtain.	Borders and shrubberies.	Top up annually.	Very easy to spread.	Can be used only if it has been fermented for 12 months. Blows away easily. Does not add nutrients.
Seaweed	Available only near the sea.	Anywhere.	Lasts only a season.	Good source of humus and trace elements.	Must be well composted before use.
Spent hops	Available from breweries.	Anywhere.	Renew annually.	Has an attractive texture and quickly improves soil structure.	Tend to blow about on windy sites.
Spent mushroom compost	Easily obtainable from mushroom farms.	Anywhere.	Renew annually.	Fine source of humus.	Very short duration; only suitable for lime-tolerant plants.
Spent tomato compost	Easily obtainable from professional growers.	Anywhere.	Renew annually.	Improves soil texture.	Blows about when dries out. High levels of fertilizer residue.
Straw	Easily available.	Most suited to vegetable gardens.	Renew annually.	Cheap enough to use copiously.	Looks messy, may carry weed seed and can only be used if supplementary nitrogenous fertilizer is added.

applied to firm (but recently cultivated) soil, before any weed seeds have had the chance to germinate. Apply the mulch evenly over the area to be covered, making sure that the mulch goes right up to the base of the plants (remember that the hardest weed to control is the one closest to the plant).

Once the mulch has been applied, give the area a light watering to settle the mulch and reduce the chance of it blowing about. This watering encourages the surface to form a 'crust' or cap, which will help to keep the planted area neat and reasonably tidy and keep the mulch in its intended position.

In all except one of the 'Garden Doctors' projects (Herne Hill was the exception) we used copious quantities of mulch whenever we could. This usually consisted of an organic material such as composted manure and bark chippings, or leaf mould.

In Cornwall, we used the material which was most readily available, shingle. We were surrounded by it, and as well as the benefits of mulching already mentioned, this shingle mulch blended in very well with the rest of the garden and gave the changes carried out by the 'Garden Doctors' team an established look very quickly.

The Camberwell communal garden had a mulch of imported gravel applied after planting, and as this gravel had also been used for making the paths, the whole appearance became one of the plants colonizing the garden rather than a deliberate planting scheme.

In other gardens, we looked at samples of man-made materials to provide a mulch: old carpet cut into strips was used in Kirsten's garden in Norwich and around Sarah and Oliver's fruit trees. We also tried well-rotted farmyard manure and plastic sheeting (recycled fertilizer bags), in order to compare them

and see which provided the best root environment for the plants.

The carpet should last about five to seven years before it rots away, and the plastic will last about twenty years if it is covered up to stop the sun's rays degrading it (only five years if not covered).

The use of mulches is not limited to plants growing in the soil. Most container-grown plants are grown in a loamless compost of one sort or another, composts which are usually dark in colour and physically very light, which means that they have a natural tendency to dry out quickly and blow away. This can be limited to a certain extent by applying a mulch to the surface. For many containerized plants, a 2.5cm (1in) layer of 3mm grit over the surface of the compost is ideal for reflecting light and heat, which helps to keep the compost cooler and prevents weed seeds germinating.

Water

We all know that plants need water in order to survive, and it comes as no surprise to learn that an ordinary plant is made up of over 90 per cent water. What may be surprising, however, is that under normal growing conditions, plants which cover a surface area of one square metre lose two litres of water a day through transpiration (nearly half a gallon per square yard).

As a practical example of this water loss, a mature lettuce transpires more than half its own weight of water every summer's day. Water stress (drought), even for relatively short periods of time, can greatly reduce the growth potential of plants. The water forms a continuous column within the plant, so if the column is broken for long periods of time, plant growth will slow down until recovery has occurred. In addition, all the chemical processes which take place in and around the plant can only do so if water is present in sufficient quantities. Water is essential for the transportation of food and chemicals around the plant.

Most plants do seem to be capable of surviving in quite inhospitable conditions once they have become established. On the Herne Hill site, however, these rules did not really apply. We were unable to mulch the troughs due to the considerations of excess weight, so we resorted to automatic watering devices to help the plants survive. Obviously, this was not possible for the individual containers on the balconies themselves, and here empty plastic drinks bottles were improvised to help provide these plants with a steady supply of water.

BRAD'S LOW-TECH WATERING DEVICE

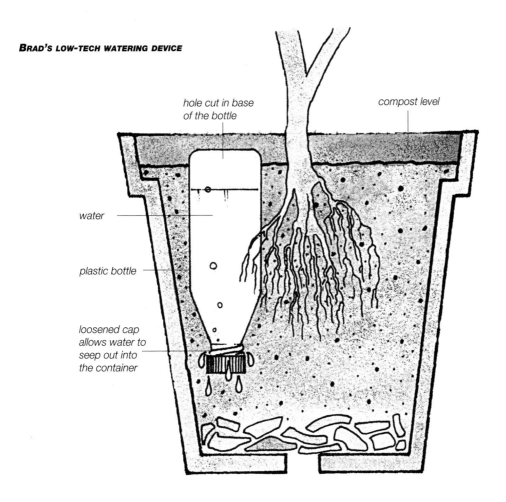

hole cut in base of the bottle

compost level

water

plastic bottle

loosened cap allows water to seep out into the container

Plant Glossary

5

Acanthus spinosa

This hardy herbaceous perennial is often described as
an 'architectural' plant. The large arching leaves are a
glossy dark green, deeply toothed, with sharp spines
on the tips of the margins. In summer, tubular white
and purple flowers are produced on bold spikes up to
1m (3ft) high. Once dead, the flower-heads can be left
on the plant over the winter, as they look very attractive
when covered in frost crystals.

Achillea millefolium **'Apricot Beauty'**

This herbaceous perennial has a compact upright
habit, with broad, finely divided, slightly hairy leaves,
dull green in colour. The lemon-yellow flowers are held
erect above the foliage in bold flat clusters upto 15cm
(6in) across. One very popular improved form is 'Gold
Plate', which has deep golden-yellow flowers.

Agapanthus umbellatus

A herbaceous perennial clump-forming plant up to
60cm (2ft) high, with deep green strap-like leaves up to

60cm (2ft) in length, and large clusters of light blue flowers produced from July onwards. It prefers full sun, and has thick fleshy roots which provide a good water store and a tolerance to drought.

Agave americana

This plant originates from Mexico. The grey/green leaves are narrow, thick and fleshy, with very tough sharp spines at the end. In late summer the flowering effect is very dramatic, with creamy-yellow bell-shaped flowers being produced on spikes of 3–5m (10–15ft) in height. The rosette bearing the flowers will usually wither with the flower stalk as it dies down. There is also a variegated form with a yellow leaf margin.

Alchemilla mollis

This herbaceous perennial originates from eastern Europe and Asia. The furry-textured light green leaves are shaped like the open palm of a child's hand, and often have a crinkled appearance to their margins. The plant develops an open centre and has a tendency towards a lax floppy growth habit. The small creamy-yellow flower-like structures are in fact bracts (modified leaves), and appear in large clusters in mid- to late summer.

Amelanchier canadensis

This is a deciduous suckering shrub with dark, almost black, thin whippy shoots. The oval-shaped mid- to dark green leaves are woolly when young, and

produce vivid autumn colours of yellow, orange and red. Brilliant white star-shaped flowers are carried in bold erect spikes in the spring before the leaves have developed, and are followed by small blackish-purple currant-like fruits in the summer and winter.

Buddleja 'Lochinch'

The buddleja is known as the butterfly bush, because its flower spikes are attractive to butterflies. This species is a deciduous shrub with silvery-green leaves and an erect habit which later becomes more spreading. The pale blue flowers are borne at the ends of the gently arching branches, with secondary flowers developing from the side-shoots immediately behind the primary flower. This plant benefits from hard pruning in early spring, after the risk of frost has gone.

Buxus sempervirens

The glossy dark green leaves of this shrub are slightly oval with a small ovate notch at the tip, and the leaves are arranged close together in pairs on the unusually shaped (square) stems. The small inconspicuous petal-less flowers, which open in spring, are pale green in colour, with yellow anthers, and smell strongly of honey.

Convolvulus cneorum

This is a slightly tender evergreen shrub of compact and low-growing bushy habit, with silvery, silky, narrow-pointed leaves on hairy silver stems. The

▲ Cortaderia selloana.

▲ Eryngium.

short-lived flowers are a soft pink in tight bud, opening to a pure white with a small golden-yellow eye in the centre, and they are produced at the tips of the shoots from May to September.

Cortaderia selloana

A bold, showy, clump-forming ornamental grass, with long narrow spear-shaped evergreen leaves with razor sharp edges to them. The flowers are carried in silvery-white plumes tinged red or purple in the autumn, held high above the arching leaves on erect pale green, almost white, stems.

Dicksonia antarctica

An attractive evergreen fern with very large frond-like leaves, originating from Southern Australia. Hardy to −5°C in the British Isles, perhaps more if provided with shelter, this slow-growing plant develops into a single furry trunk made up of the fibrous remains of old leaf stalks, which helps to give it a palm-like appearance. The large fern fronds are finely divided and up to 2m (6ft) long, glossy mid-green on the upper surface, and a dull matt green beneath.

Digitalis ferruginea

This superb perennial foxglove forms a clump of strap-like leaves with a toothed margin, mid-green in colour, and covered with soft hairs on the underside. The clear pale yellow flowers have a pattern of brown net-like markings on the inside and are carried on tall erect flower spikes up to 1m (3ft) or more in height.

This plant is relatively short-lived and must be replaced every third or fourth year.

Eryngium

This herbaceous perennial at first glance looks like a cross between a holly and a thistle. It has tough, spiny, toothed leaves which vary in colour from dark green through to silvery-blue, depending upon the species. The flowers look very much like teasel heads – they are a metallic silvery-blue, with a collar of broad spines at their base, and are held on strong wiry stems above the leaves.

Festuca glauca

This low growing, tussock-forming little grass with tufts of blue-grey leaves is a valuable garden plant for a number of positions. It maintains its growth pattern and colour throughout the winter, and copes very well on windy, exposed sites. The purple flower spikes are carried above the leaves in the summer, and will remain to provide decoration long after flowering has finished.

Genista aetnensis

This is an elegant rounded shrub, with many slender, drooping, bright-green branches which are practically leafless. The tough, sparse leaves are mid-green in colour and strap-like, with fine white silky hairs. The heavily scented pea-like flowers are a golden yellow colour and produced in large quantities on the tips of shoots in mid-summer.

Geranium pratense

This low-growing perennial has a dome-shaped spreading habit, with deeply lobed leaves with a scalloped margin. The saucer-shaped flowers have five petals, and are violet-blue with clearly marked red veins within each petal. In the autumn the leaves turn orange before dying down for the winter.

Humulus lupulus

An attractive self-supporting herbaceous perennial climber with thin bristly twining stems; the bristly leaves are toothed around the margins and have deep lobes (like sycamore). The flowers are insignificant, but the fruit clusters are quite attractive in the autumn. The most popular form is 'Aureus', a clone with soft golden-yellow leaves, stems and fruits.

Hydrangea petiolaris

This vigorous, hardy deciduous climber, which supports itself by aerial roots, is grown for its large flat clusters of creamy-white flowers produced on the shoot tips of lateral branches. The rich dark green leaves are oval in shape, tapering to a point, with the margins of the leaves having small teeth. The underside of the leaf is pale green and covered in downy felt.

Laurus nobilis

A hardy evergreen small tree or large shrub, originating from the Mediterranean. This plant thrives in coastal regions, though the leaves may be scorched by persistent cold winds. They are often grown as a clipped and shaped specimen or as standard or half-standard in containers. The dark-green, glossy, sharply pointed strap-like leaves are aromatic and are used in cooking.

Lavandula angustifolia

This popular plant has narrow aromatic, silver-grey leaves covered with fine felt-like hairs, which are very effective for preventing moisture loss. The small tube-like flowers are carried in narrow clusters (spikes), on tough square stems. The most commonly grown form is 'Hidcote', which has strongly scented deep purple-blue flowers and a compact bushy habit.

Lonicera

These attractive twining climbers have fragrant flowers which are tubular, opening out to a broad mouth. The colours range from white through pale yellow to gold, pink and scarlet. The leaves vary in shape from broadly oval to almost circular, and from pale to mid-green in colour, carried in pairs on thin twiggy stems. *L. periclymenum* hybrids are very popular.

Nicotiana

This tall, attractive bedding plant is grown for its extravagant display of tube-like flowers, produced in large clusters. There are a multitude of flower colours, the most popular being white, cream, yellow and crimson. The new flowers open in the evening, and

▲ **Zantedeschia aethiopica.**

▲ Rosa rugosa.

most are heavily scented. The leaves are mid-green, oval-shaped with a pointed tip, and are slightly sticky to the touch.

Nymphaea

The hardy water-lilies, which flower over a long period in the summer, have large, tough, but elegant blooms which are sometimes sweetly scented. Most varieties are long-lived and require little detailed attention, only routine maintenance. The flowers and leaves rise from a thick rootstock anchored securely in the mud by long tough roots. The round or heart-shaped leaves are a reddish-green, with a shiny, leathery upper surface. The saucer-shaped flowers have several rows of petals, with the outer layer opening out almost flat as the flower opens fully, to show conspicuous golden or orange stamens in the centre.

Papaver

A genus of annual, biennial and perennial herbaceous flowering plants, with deeply lobed, hairy, grey-green leaves. Poppy flowers are produced from midsummer through to mid-autumn, and generally have broad, overlapping petals. These become narrow at the base to form a characteristic cup or bowl shape. Their colour is predominantly red, but yellow, orange, pink and white are also quite common.

Perovskia atriplicifolia

An attractive deciduous shrub, with thin grey-white stems, carrying narrowly oval, grey-green aromatic foliage. The violet-blue flowers are produced in long slender spikes on the tips of the shoots. The most commonly seen variety is 'Blue Spire', with larger blue flowers and deeply cut grey-green leaves. This plant will be frosted down to ground level in winter but grows up again from the base in the spring.

Phormium tenax

This clump-forming evergreen perennial has bold sword-shaped leaves, deep green in colour, with a tough leathery texture. When the plant has established, dull orange flowers are borne in summer on large erect spikes up to 3m (10ft) high, followed by scimitar-shaped seed capsules. There are also a number of cultivars with variegated or purple foliage.

Phyllostachys nigra

The black bamboo has thick canes which turn the colour and sheen of ebony as they age, but the plant must be grown in full sun for this to happen. The glossy green foliage and arching habit of the plant make it a pleasing ornamental plant. Although it thrives in full sun it struggles in a dry situation.

Pittisporum

A large evergreen shrub suitable for milder or coastal districts. Although grown chiefly for their attractive foliage, some have small, colourful, fragrant bell-shaped flowers with spreading petals. *Pittosporum tenuifolium* is the most commonly grown, mainly because it is one of the hardier species. It has pale green oblong leaves with very prominent wavy margins, arranged on thin bluish-black branches. The small flowers which appear in the spring are a chocolate-purple in colour and have the gentle aroma of warm honey.

Populus alba

A common deciduous tree with a broad spreading habit, dark grey-green fissured bark, and young shoots which are covered with a thick white felt. The main attraction is the foliage: the dark green leaves have a silver down on the underside, and turn golden yellow in the autumn. There is a very attractive golden cultivar, 'Richardii', much slower growing, which has small golden leaves with white undersides.

Pyracantha

This is a versatile evergreen shrub grown for its attractive foliage, fruit and flowers. It is useful for hedging, as a wall shrub or as a free-standing specimen in the garden. The large clusters of small white or pale pink blooms are produced in the early summer, to be followed by huge clusters of round fruits in the autumn, coloured yellow, orange or red depending upon the cultivar grown.

Rosa rugosa

This is a very tough, dense and vigorous rose, growing up to 2m (6ft), with shoots densely covered with fine bristly thorns, and deeply-veined, glossy dark-green leaves, which turn orange in the autumn.

The large single deep pink flowers have an open cup-shape, with a bright golden-yellow centre; these are followed in the autumn by large round bright red hips.

Rosmarinus officinalis

This most popular of aromatic shrubs has an erect, open habit, with narrow aromatic evergreen leaves. The flowers, which look a little like small lobelia flowers, and range in colour from white, through to blues, pinks and mauves, are produced in small clusters at the leaf joints.

Ruta

A hardy aromatic evergreen perennial known to have been grown in England since 1652. The blue-green leaves are roughly oval in shape, and deeply divided to give a fern-like appearance. They give off a pungent aromatic odour. The small yellow flowers are carried on thick blue-green stems in large flat clusters from mid- to late summer. 'Jackman's Blue' is the variety most often grown.

Salvia officinalis

The true sage has dull green leaves which have a roughly textured surface, often with a reddish tinge to them. The tubular flowers open into a funnel shape at the mouth, and are produced on spikes at the tips of the stems or in small groups from the leaf joints.
S. officinalis has some very interesting leaf forms, the purple 'Purpurescens' being the most common.

▲ Sedum *'Autumn Joy' before coming into flower.*

▲ Vitis coignetiae.

Sedum spectabile 'Autumn Joy'

This plant forms a rounded bushy plant 30-50cm (12-20in) high with erect, stout, unbranched stems. The grey-green leaves are fleshy and somewhat toothed. The bright pink flowers are carried in broad flat clusters 10-15cm (7-6in) wide, and appear in late summer and early autumn. This plant likes full sun and fertile soil. It is a good companion for ornamental grasses and is suitable for perennial borders and for many other garden situations.

Sinarundinaria nitida

This is a frost-hardy, clump-forming bamboo, with small pointed, mid-green leaves, giving a delicate effect. The dark purplish stalks which shoot up 2-3m (6-9ft), are very straight in the first year and do not branch at all until the second season. This plant prefers shade and may also be used for screening.

Solanum crispum

A most attractive wall shrub which makes a splendid display, with its large clusters of small star-shaped purple-blue flowers with a yellow centre. The leaves have a glossy dark green upper surface with a paler underside, and turn yellow in the autumn. The erect stems are a bright glossy green even through the winter, and are valued for their winter stem effect.

Stipa tenuissima

This grass has very narrow yellow-green foliage which grows in an erect fashion, and elegant drooping flower-heads in midsummer. It is among the most delicate of all the grasses and when planted in drifts is said to resemble billowing clouds or rolling ocean waves. It will grow well in ordinary soil and does best in full sun.

Taxus baccata

A hardy evergreen conifer which usually has an open spreading habit. It has small, dark, glossy green leaves with a slightly paler underside. The bark is usually a fresh orange-brown when young, turning a dull grey-brown with age. The female flowers produce cup-shaped red fleshy fruits in the autumn (this flesh is the only part of the plant which is not poisonous).

Thymus

A hardy evergreen sub-shrub, with aromatic leaves. Some species are mat-forming and prostrate, while others may grow up to form small shrubby plants with tough thin twiggy stems. The small narrow oval-shaped leaves are usually grey-green and sometimes hairy, arranged close together on thin twig-like branches. Some species have a mat-forming habit with small strap-like grey-green leaves, held just above ground level, making a dense carpet.

Tropaeolum

A trailing plant with short broadly trumpet-shaped flowers. The smooth leaves are almost circular with a crinkled edge, and mid- to light-green in colour. The annual species, including the familiar nasturtium, are suitable for growing in pots in hanging baskets, and the climbing perennials are useful for covering trellis work, or for growing through small trees or shrubs.

Verbena bonariensis

This plant is a native of South America, growing well in wet fields and on waste ground in full sun. The erect stems reach up the 1m (3ft) in height, and flat clusters of purple flowers are produced on the tips from midsummer onwards. In hard winters this plant will be killed off, but because of its habit of self-seeding, large numbers of plants usually emerge in the same spot the following spring.

Viburnum rhytidophyllum

A large evergreen shrub with thick leathery deeply-veined leaves. The white flowers are clustered together to form a mop head, some of which produce brightly coloured fruits in the autumn. This plant is much favoured for its more practical qualities: a tolerance to pollution (particularly exhaust fumes) and its use as a noise-absorbent barrier once established.

Vinca

These hardy, invasive plants are suitable as evergreen ground cover or as trailing plants in containers. The small 3cm (1.5in) flowers are tubular, with five angular or rounded petals opening out flat, from late spring until early autumn. *V. major* is a spreading plant with glossy dark green leaves, trailing stems and purple-blue flowers. There is a slower growing variety, 'Elegantissima', which has pale green and white variegated leaves.

Vitis coignetiae

This remarkable plant is the finest of all ornamental vines, and is a vigorous species often reaching 20m (60ft) high. The young stems are ribbed and covered with a loose grey felty down. The large thick leaves are mid-green and covered with rust-red hairs on the underside. The large leaves, up to 30cm (12in) across, are heart-shaped and they turn yellow, orange-red and eventually purple-crimson in the autumn.

Zantedeschia aethiopica

Originating from South Africa, and grown for its display of unusual pure white tubular flowers, 20cm (8in) long, with a conspicuous yellow spike in the centre, which are carried singly on a 45cm (18in) stem in spring and summer. The large glossy dark green leaves are an 'arrowhead' shape and are carried above the ground on a tough wiry stalk. There is a hardier form called 'Crowborough'.

▶ *(Following spread)* **Achillea millefolium *'Apricot Beauty'*.**

List of Suppliers and
Useful Information

PLANTS AND SEEDS:

Angus White
Architectural Plants
Cooks Farm
Nuthurst
Horsham
West Sussex
RH13 6LH
Tel: (01403) 891 772

Suppliers of exotic and architectural plants,
as used in the
Balham and Sussex gardens.

Pauline Brown
Buckingham Nurseries
14 Tingewick Road
Buckingham
Buckinghamshire
MK18 4AE
Tel: (01280) 813 556

Suppliers and producers of a wide range of
hardy plants, as used in the
Buckinghamshire garden.

Countryside Flowers
Chatteris Road
Somersham
Cambridgeshire
PE17 3DN
Tel: (01487) 841 322

Growers and distributors of a wide range of
native plant and grass seeds, as used in the
Buckinghamshire and Norwich gardens.

Four Seasons Nurseries
Forcutt St Mary
Norwich
Norfolk
NR16 1JT
Tel: (01508) 488 344

Clive Shelton
Hardy Exotics
Gilly Lane
Whitecross
Penzance
Cornwall
TR20 8BZ
Tel: (01736) 740 660

Suppliers of exotic plants, as used in the
Balham, Cornwall and Sussex gardens.
(Mail order offered. Send four 1st class
stamps for catalogue.)

Kennedys Garden Centres Ltd
Kennedy House
11 Crown Row
Bracknell
Berkshire
RG12 0TH
Tel: (01344) 860 022

A long-established garden centre chain
with outlets in the south-east and
Midlands. Plants supplied for the Balham
and Camberwell gardens.

Lawrence Greasley
Plant Magic
Woodmoss Lane
Scarisbrick
Ormskirk
Lancashire
L40 9HJ

Ian Roger
R. V. Roger Ltd
The Nurseries
Pickering
North Yorkshire
YO18 7HG
Tel: (01751) 472 226

Producers of a wide range of British
grown hardy plants, as used in the
Norwich and Balham gardens.
(Mail order service.)

John Amand
Jacques Amand Nurseries
Clamp Hill
Stanmore
Middlesex
HA7 3JS
Tel: (0181) 954 8138

Suppliers of a wide range of bulbs
including many rare species.

Lynne Wainwright
Burford Garden Company
Shilton Road
Burford
Oxfordshire
OX18 4PA
Tel: (01993) 823 117

Emorsgate Seeds
The Pea Mill
Market Lane
Terrington St Clements
Norfolk
PE34 4HR
Tel: (01553) 829 028

Growers and distributors of a wide range of
native plant and grass seeds, as used in the
Buckinghamshire and Cotswolds gardens.

John Cook
Green Farm Plants
Green Farm
Bentley
Farnham
Surrey
GU10 5JX
Tel: (01420) 23202

Hoecroft Plants
Severals Grange
Holt Road
Wood Norton
Dereham
Norfolk
Tel: (01362) 684 206

Suppliers of specialist ornamental grasses,
variegated and coloured foliage plants, as
used in the Cornwall garden.

Isabelle Rogerso
Rolawn (Turf growers) Ltd
Elvington
York
North Yorkshire
YO4 5AR
Tel: (01904) 608 661

Turf manufacturers and inventors of the
turf-laying system, as used in the
Cotswolds garden.

Suttons Seeds Ltd
Hele Road
Torquay
Devon
TQ2 7QL
Tel: (01803) 614 455

Growers and distributors of an extensive
range of seeds, as used in the Norwich,
Camberwell and Cotswolds gardens.

MATERIALS:

Pottery

Lesley Jones
APTA Pottery
Dencora Way
Leacon Road
Fairwood Business Park
Ashford
Kent
PN23 4FH
Tel: (01233) 621 090

Importers and suppliers of Thai terracotta pots, as used in the Camberwell garden.

C. H. Brannam Ltd
Roundswell Industrial Estate
Oakwood Close
Barnstaple
North Devon
EX31 3NJ
Tel: (01271) 43035

Manufacturers of hand-made terracotta pots and garden ornaments, as used in the Herne Hill garden.

Jane Lancia
Whichford Pottery
Whichford
Nr Shipton-on-Stour
Warwickshire
CV36 5PG
Tel: (01608) 684 416

Manufacturers of hand-made terracotta pots and garden ornaments, as used in the Camberwell and Cotswolds gardens.

Lighting

Outdoor Lighting
Unit C
Agent Court
Hook Rise South
Tolworth
Surrey
KT6 7LD
Tel: (0181) 974 2211

Suppliers of Morph spotlights and Nimbus recessed uplighters, as used in the Crouch End garden.

Wattle Hurdles

Graham Mead
1 Elm Cottage
Twyford
Winchester
Hampshire
SO21 1QQ
Tel: (01962) 712 916

Producers of traditional wattle, as used in the Cotswolds and Norwich gardens.

Ropes

Mr Leach
Splicing & Allied Services
Eldorado Works
Drake Avenue
Gresham Road
Staines
Middlesex
TW18 2AP
Tel: (01784) 464 447

Manufacturers and suppliers of ropes, as used in the Norwich garden.

Window Boxes and Plant Hangers

Chelsea Herbalist Ltd
32 New Broadway
Tarring Road
Worthing
West Sussex
BN11 4HP
Tel: (01903) 210 225

Suppliers of secure plant hangers, as used in the Herne Hill garden.

IKEA
(Head Office U.K.)
Store number 141
2 Drury Way
North Circular Road
London
NW10 OTH
Tel: (0181) 208 5600

Suppliers of galvanized window boxes, as used in the Herne Hill garden.

Garden Furniture

Habitat U.K. Ltd
(Head Office)
The Heals Building
196 Tottenham Court Road
London
W1P 9LD
Tel: (0171) 631 3880

Garden Sculpture

Sunna Wathen
102 Arodene Road
London
SW2 2BH
Tel: (0181) 671 8791

Suppliers of tree sculpture, as used in the Berkshire garden.

Garden Irrigation and Pumps

Gardena (U.K.) Ltd
7 Denhams Court
Denhams Lane
Letchworth
Hertfordshire
SG6 1BD
Tel: (01462) 475 000

Suppliers of garden products and watering systems, as used in the Herne Hill garden.

Lotus Water Products (Trade only)
PO Box 36
Junction Street
Burnley
Lancashire
BB12 0NA
Tel: (01282) 420 771 (for details of local stockists)

Suppliers of pumps and water garden products, as used in the Cornwall and Crouch End gardens.

Trade & DIY Products
The Pump House
Hazelwood Road
Duffield
Derby
DE56 4DQ
Tel: (01332) 842 685
Fax: (01332) 842 806

Suppliers of hydromat capillary matting, as used in the Herne Hill garden. (Full mail order service.)

Fertilizers and Mulches

Levington Horticulture
Papermill Lane
Bramford
Ipswich
Suffolk
IP8 4BZ
Tel: (01473) 830492 (for details of stockists)

Suppliers of woodland chipped bark, as used in the Cornwall garden.

Robert Delany
Rich Earth
London Conservation Services Ltd
80 York Way
London
N1 9AG
Tel: (0171) 278 6606

Miracle Garden Care Ltd
Tel: (0990) 301 010 (for details of osmocote slow-release fertilizer stockists)

William Sinclair Holdings
Firth Road
Lincoln
Lincolnshire
LN6 7AH
Tel: (01522) 537 561

Suppliers of Mix 'N' Mulch, as used in the Cornwall garden. Stockists of the Arthur Bowers compost – a natural alternative to peat for soil conditioning and mulching. 100% organic.

Building Supplies

Harcros Timber & Building Supplies Ltd (Head Office)
Harcros House
1 Central Road
Worcester Park
Surrey
KT4 8DN
Tel: (0181) 255 2253

Hanson Bricks
Stewartby Works
Stewartby
Bedford
Bedfordshire
MK43 9LZ
Tel: (0900) 258258

Suppliers of Canturbury Multi Stock, as used in the Berkshire garden.

**Civil Engineering
Developments Ltd**
728 London Road
West Thurrock
Grays
Essex
RM20 3LU
Tel: (01708) 867 237

*Suppliers of footpath gravel, as used in
the Nottinghamshire garden.*

Tools and Equipment

**Black & Decker
(Head Office)**
210 Bath Road
Slough
Berkshire
SL1 3YD
Tel: (01753) 511 234

JC Bamford Excavators Ltd
Rocester
Uttoxeter
Staffordshire
ST14 5JP
Tel: (01889) 590 312

**Melanie Wiggins
Builders Merchant Federation**
15 Soho square
London
W1V 6HL
Tel: (0171) 439 1753 (for details of
local building contractors)

H H S Hire Service Group plc
25 Willow Lane
Mitcham
Surrey
CR4 4TS
Tel: (0181) 260 3100

**Fiskars UK Ltd
(Head Office)**
Bridgend Business Centre
Bridgend
Mid Glamorgan
Wales
CS31 SXJ
Tel: (01656) 655 595

Paint

Hammerite Products Ltd
Proudhoe
Northumberland
NE4Z 6LP
Tel: (01661) 830 000

John Oliver Paints
33 Pembridge Road
London
W11 3HG
Tel: (0171) 221 6466

*Suppliers of Persian Peacock and
Imperial Chinese Yellow paints, as used in
the Crouch End garden.*

Landscaping Organisations

The following landscaping
organisations regulate their
members to ensure a high
standard of service and
workmanship, and will be happy
to advise you of local members.

**British Association of
Landscape Industries
(BALI)**
Landscape House
9 Henry Street
Keighley
West Yorkshire
BD21 3DR
Tel: (01535) 606 139

Landscape Institute
6/7 Bernard Mews
London
SW11 1QU
Tel: (0171) 738 9166

Society of Garden Designers
6 Borough Road
Kingston-upon-Thames
Surrey
KT2 6DB
Tel: (0181) 974 9483

Courses in Landscape Construction and Design

Part-time and full-time courses are offered by many colleges in Britain, including those listed below. Your local library and nearest Job Centre should have details of those available in your area.

Askham Bryan College
Askham Bryan
York
YO2 3PR
Tel: (01904) 702 121

Berkshire College of Agriculture
Hall Place
Burchetts Green
Nr Maidenhead
Berkshire
SL6 6QR
Tel: (01628) 824 444

Brinsbury College of Agriculture and Horticulture
North Heath
Pulborough
West Sussex
RH20 1DL
Tel: (01798) 873 832

Broomfield College
Morley
Derby
DE7 6DN
Tel: (01332) 831 345

Capel Manor Horticulture and Environment Centre
Bullsmoor Lane
Enfield
Middlesex
EN1 4RQ
Tel: (0181) 366 4442

Duchy College of Agriculture and Horticulture
West Cornwall Centre
Pool
Redruth
Cornwall
TR15 3RD
Tel: (01209) 710 077

Easton College
Easton
Norwich
NR9 5DX
Tel: (01603) 742 105

Inchbold School of Design
32 Eccleston Square
London
SW1
Tel: (0171) 730 5508

Lancashire College of Agriculture and Horticulture
Myerscough Hall
Bilsborrow
Preston
Lancashire
PR3 0RY
Tel: (01995) 640 611

Writtle University College
Writtle
Chelmsford
Essex
CM1 3RR
Tel: (01245) 420 705

Correspondence Courses in Garden Design

English Gardening School
Chelsea Physic Garden
66 Royal Hospital Road
London
SW3 4HS
Tel: (0171) 352 4347

Horticultural Correspondence College
Little Norton Farmhouse
Lacock
Chippenham
Wiltshire
SN15 2NF
Tel: (01249) 730 326

A comprehensive list of colleges and outline details of the courses they run can be found in *The Gardener's Yearbook 1996*, published by Macmillan.

Further Reading &
Acknowledgements

Best Plants for Your Garden by Susan Berry and Steve Bradley, Lorenz Books, 1996

The Complete Book of Patio and Container Gardening by Robin Williams, Mary-Jane Hopes and Robin Templar Williams, Ward Lock, 1992

The Complete Guide to Gardening with Containers by Susan Berry and Steve Bradley, Collins & Brown, 1995

Dictionary of Plant Names by Allen J. Coombes, Hamlyn Books, 1994

The Low-Maintenance Garden by Graham Rose, Francis Lincoln, 1983

Ornamental Grasses, Bamboos, Rushes and Sedges by Nigel J. Taylor, Ward Lock, 1994

Plants for Dry Gardens by Jane Taylor, Frances Lincoln, 1993

RHS Gardeners Encyclopaedia of Plants and Flowers edited by Chris Brickell, Dorling Kindersley, 1989

Seaside Gardening by F. W. Shepherd, RHS/Cassell, 1990

Acknowledgements

Thanks to David Edgar (series producer) for giving us the opportunity to work on the 'Garden Doctors' series, and to everyone else at Flashback Television, particularly Serena Cross, Ann Lalic and Jonathan Lubert (production manager), as well as all the helpful people we met while we were making the series.

In putting the book together, we are also very grateful to Katy Carrington at Boxtree for her editorial organisation, Andrea Jones for her excellent photography, Nick Pearson for his illustrations and Bobby Birchall at DW Design.

For help with the hard work and technical skills, special thanks to the following:

The Principal, staff and students
Berkshire College of Agriculture
Hall Place
Burchetts Green
Nr Maidenhead
Berkshire
SL6 6QR
Tel: (01628) 82444

The Principal, staff and students
Duchy College of Agriculture and Horticulture
West Cornwall Centre
Pool
Redruth
Cornwall
TR15 3RD
Tel: (01209) 710 077

The Principal, staff and students
Pershore College of Horticulture
Pershore
Worcestershire
WR10 3JP
Tel: (01386) 552 443

The Principal, staff and students
Broomfield College
Morley
Derby
DE7 6DN
Tel: (01332) 831 345

The Principal, staff and students
Easton College
Norwich
NR9 5DX
Tel: (01603) 742 105

Trevor Webb
Spider's Gardening Services
26 Fort Road
Gosport
Hampshire
PO12 2AR
Tel: (01705) 529 218

Manor Farm Nurseries
Hellidon
Charwelton
Northampshire

Index

(Numbers in italics refer to illustrations. Where appropriate, the botanical name of a plant has been followed by the common name.)